A Guide to
FRESHWATER
FISH

A Guide to
FRESHWATER
FISH

by
Jiří Cihař
Illustrated by
Libuše and Jaromír Knotek

TREASURE PRESS

Text by Jiří Čihař
Illustrations by Libuše and Jaromír Knotek
Graphic design by L. Knotková
Translated by Margot Schierlová
First published in Great Britain in 1991.
Designed and produced by Aventinum for Treasure Press
Michelin House, 81 Fulham Road
London SW3 6RB
Copyright © 1991 Aventinum, Praha
ISBN 1 85051 595 6
Printed in Czechoslovakia by Svoboda Praha
3/07/23/51-01

Contents

Introduction

The animals that this book describes belong to two vertebrate classes— cyclostomes or roundmouths (Cyclostomata), which are jawless aquatic vertebrates, and bony fishes (Osteichthyes). The former class, which in European fresh water is represented only by the lamprey family (Petromyzonidae), have a permanently cartilaginous skeleton, no paired fins and in their adult stage a round, toothed sucking mouth. Except for the most primitive species, the sturgeons (Acipenseridae), most of the members of the second class, the bony fishes, have a fully ossified skeleton. Apart from minor exceptions they all have well developed paired fins and proper jaws, which may or may not be armed with teeth.

About two hundred cyclostome and bony, true fish species occur in European lakes and rivers. This relatively concise book is too short for a full description of the appearance, biology and distribution of all of them and so, on the following pages, we shall deal with only the commonest and most widespread species. Related species of lesser significance, or those with limited geographical ranges, will be mentioned only briefly.

The geographical range covered by the book is Europe, i.e. the mainland and islands bounded by the Arctic and Atlantic Oceans, the Mediterranean, the western shores of the Black Sea and the Sea of Azov, the Caucasus, the northern shores of the Caspian Sea, the river Ural and the Ural mountains.

In addition to those cyclostomes and bony, true fishes which spend the whole of their life in fresh water, the reader will also be introduced to marine fishes, which breed in fresh water, and to others whose true home is the sea, but which tolerate brackish and fresh water and are sometimes found there.

Fish as aquatic vertebrates

Fish are the most familiar and conspicuous inhabitants of fresh water in Europe, although they share this environment with many other animals and plants. Every type of water body has its own special community of aquatic organisms, and every organism has its own clearly defined niche within the habitat. Successful co-existence in water requires the maintenance of a delicate balance between the various groups of organisms which inhabit it. This gives rise to the formation of complex food webs in which the smaller and weaker links provide food for the bigger and stronger elements. Microscopic bacteria and unicellular plants are food for zooplankton and predatory insect larvae, which in turn may be eaten by fish.

In a typical freshwater habitat, fish-eating birds and mammals form the top of the food web.

Conditions for life in water and on dry land differ fundamentally in several respects. Water is much denser than air. Aquatic animals are consequently exposed to greater pressure than land animals and their movements must overcome significantly greater resistance. However, since their density is roughly the same as the weight of water, they are usually buoyant.

Like air, there are certain basic properties which water must possess if life is to survive in it. These include a suitable temperature, together with an adequate supply of dissolved oxygen and other organic and inorganic substances.

The water temperature is particularly important during the breeding season and determines, for example, the length of time embryos take to develop. It also greatly influences the amount of planktonic life present in the water.

On a day-to-day basis the temperature of a body of fresh water will vary much less than the temperature of the surrounding air. On the other hand, the oxygen content of air remains roughly the same, whatever the temperature, whereas in water it rapidly dwindles when the temperature rises. During both day and night, aquatic animals respire, taking in oxygen from the water and releasing carbon dioxide into it. Green aquatic plants take up the carbon dioxide during photosynthetic assimilation and, together with water, convert it to sugars and other organic substances, whilst at the same time releasing oxygen into the water. Photosynthesis takes place only during the daytime and at night, plants also respire and take up oxygen from the water.

In running water, the oxygen content is constantly replenished by mixing with the air, but in stagnant water, and in warm weather especially, the amount of dissolved oxygen sometimes falls so low that fish and other sensitive organisms literally suffocate. Of course, different species have different oxygen requirements; for instance, fish living in torrential mountain streams need far more oxygen than fish living in slow-flowing or stagnant lowland waters.

As with many other aquatic animals, fish breathe by means of gills. They take in water through their mouth and let it out by opening their gill covers (opercula), after the richly vascularized branchial (gill) lamellae have extracted the oxygen and released it into the blood stream. Species living in poorly oxygenated water often have accessory respiratory organs. The Weatherfish, for example, absorbs oxygen through its intestine, Eels can absorb oxygen via their skin and in the Mudminnow the swim-bladder also takes up oxygen.

The swim-bladder enables fish to swim at any depth they wish. Gaseous exchange between the blood and the swim-bladder regulates their specific weight at different depths. By releasing gas from the posterior part of the bladder into the anterior part and *vice versa*, they can quickly change position and swim downwards or upwards. Fish which live on the bottom (e.g. bullheads) do not possess a swim-bladder.

The fish's organs of locomotion are its fins. Most fishes have paired pectoral and ventral fins and single dorsal, caudal and anal fins. Sometimes one pair of fins may be missing (Eels, for instance, have no ventral fins), while in other cases the dorsal or caudal fin may be absent (some marine species).

The fins are reinforced with soft, branching rays and hard rays like spines. The position, shape and size of the fins and in particular the number of rays are important in identification.

The body is usually covered with scales. If the protruding parts of the scales are smooth, the scales are described as cycloid; if they feel rough like fine sandpaper, they are known as ctenoid scales. Along the sides of their body and head, most fishes have a curious sensory organ known as the lateral line, which enables them to perceive pressure waves produced in the water by the movements of other creatures or by obstacles. This 'remote sensing' organ enables fish to find their way about

 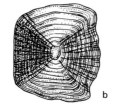

Scales: a— ctenoid, b — cycloid

with complete ease, even in turbid water and in the dark.

As to the shape of the body fishes are perfectly adapted for life in water. The commonest is the fusiform, streamlined body particularly characteristic of fast swimmers. The Pike, a familiar predator in fresh water, has a dart-like form, whereas the Eel has a long, serpentine body bordered posteriorly, above and below, by a continuous dorsal, caudal and anal fin. Fish inhabiting sluggish or stagnant water usually have a high, flat-sided body (e.g. the Bream and the Bitterling).

The body colour is often very variable. Some fish, e.g. Trout, Minnows and Perch, are brightly coloured when seen out of water, while others have more sober hues or only one colour. All European freshwater fishes have a dark back, lighter (in some cases silvery or golden) sides and a white, cream or yellow belly. Apart from a few exceptions, the unpaired fins are grey and the paired fins are reddish, orange or yellow. In general, however, the colouring of the surface of the body always serves a specific purpose. A brightly coloured Trout against a background of variegated pebbles in a mountain stream is just as inconspicuous as a dark-banded Perch among roots and branches in the water near the bank, or a green-spotted Pike lying in wait for prey in dense aquatic vegetation.

As among other animals, various colour aberrations also occur among fish. The best known are albino forms—fish completely lacking in any kind of pigment. Xanthorism—yellow or red colouring known in goldfish, orfes, veiltails and many other aquarium species—is another colour aberration. Completely black (melanic) forms, in which black pigment cells (melanophores) are distributed over the whole surface of the fish's body, are less frequent.

In the spawning season, male cyprinid fishes (and in some species the fe-

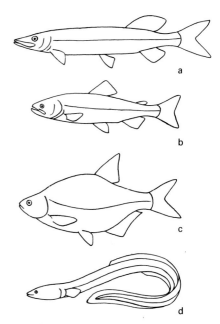

Shapes of fish bodies: a — sagittal, b — fusiform, c — flat-sided, d — serpentine

males also) develop a spawning 'rash' on their head, sides and fins, in the form of conical horny wartlike tubercles which make the skin feel very rough. Their purpose is probably to stimulate the other partner mechanically during spawning and they always disappear after spawning is over.

The various species of freshwater fish differ markedly in their size, as well as in their form and colouring. The smallest native European freshwater fish is the Moderlieschen (*Leucaspius delineatus*), which measures no more than 5—6 cm and weighs only 2—3 g. The Bitterling (*Rhodeus sericeus*) is a little more robust and so are the slim-bodied loaches (*Cobitis*). Smaller than all these, however, is the Mosquito Fish (*Gambusia affinis*), which comes from North America, but has been introduced to many parts of Europe; the males of this species are only 3.5 cm long and the females not more than 6 cm.

The largest European freshwater fish, the Great Sturgeon or Beluga (*Huso huso*), inhabits rivers flowing into the Black Sea, the Caspian Sea and the Sea of Azov and some of the rivers of the Adriatic. In exceptional cases it can measure up to 5 m and weigh up to 1,500 kg. The other sturgeon species can also grow to huge proportions. Another giant among European fishes is the Wels or European Catfish (*Silurus glanis*), which occasionally measures about 3 m and can weigh over 100 kg. Record size Pikes (*Esox lucius*), like Danube Salmon (*Hucho hucho*), can measure over 1.5 m and weigh 35—40 kg. Sea Trout (*Salmo trutta trutta*), Pike-perch (*Stizostedion*), Carp (*Cyprinus carpio*) and other species also grow to a generous size, especially in large valley reservoirs. Cases are known in which Carp over 1 m long and weighing over 30 kg have been caught.

The age of a fish is generally related to its size, and can be determined relatively exactly using the structure of the scales and some of the bones (e.g. the vertebrae or the opercular bones). The bones and scales not only tell us the fish's age, but also the rate at which it grew in previous years. Being poikilo-thermic animals (with a variable body temperature), fish grow periodically, i.e. at different rates according to the season. Summer growth increments are seen on the scales and bones as lighter concentric bands, whereas winter increments take the form of narrow dark lines. If we count the number of dark winter rings on a scale or a vertebra under a magnifying glass or microscope, the result will tell us the number of winters the fish has lived through, i.e. its age. Similarly, the distance of the individual winter circles from the centre of the scale or vertebra allows us to calculate how fast the fish grew in previous years. Age and growth rate can likewise

be caculated from abraded smooth sections through the otoliths, which are chalky granules in the fish's inner ear concerned with balance.

Unlike warm-blooded vertebrates, fish continue to grow for the whole of their life, although the rate at which they grow decreases with advancing age. Small species have a life span of only a few years, whereas large fish such as Carp, Catfish, Trout and Pike, etc, can live for dozens of years. The oldest known Brown Trout attained an age of 49 years, while the oldest Eel, which was kept in a small pool belonging to a Prague insurance company, died of old age at 68 years.

Every angler knows that some fish are caught in swift mountain streams and others in deep, slow-flowing lowland rivers. Individual species thus have specific environmental requirements, and it follows that running water can be divided into 'fish zones' named after the typical fish inhabitants.

The mountain reaches of streams and rivers, with fast currents, rapids, waterfalls and clear, deep pools with cold, well-oxygenated water, are known as the trout zone, because here the trout is the most important fish. In addition to the Brown Trout, this zone is inhabited by tiny Bullheads, Minnows and often by Stone Loaches. Submontane streams and rivers have a different character. Here there is more water, the gradient is more gradual and the current is slower. In this zone we will sometimes encounter trout and other fishes of the higher reaches, but the typical fish is the Grayling and it is therefore known as the grayling zone. Further downstream we often come across Chub, Dace, Gudgeon, Burbot and even Pike. The characteristic fish of large, deep, fast-flowing rivers at low altitudes is the Barbel and this type of water is therefore known as the barbel zone. Slow, deep lowland rivers with meanders and deep pools harbour many fishes of the carp family; such stretches

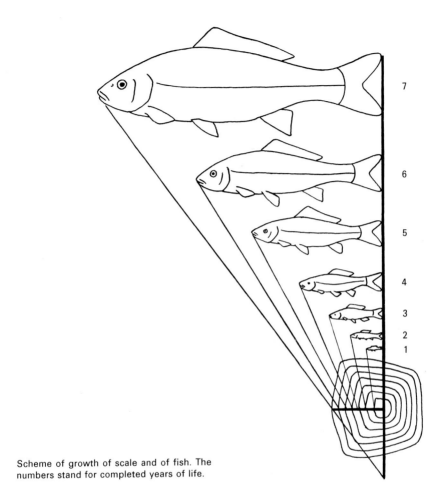

Scheme of growth of scale and of fish. The numbers stand for completed years of life.

are known as the bream zone, after the most typical—and in some places the commonest—fish to be found there.

As you might expect, the various fish zones are not necessarily all represented in *every* river and their order is also frequently changed — mainly through the interference of man. For instance, a secondary trout or grayling zone is often formed at the foot of a deep dam, in places where there was once a barbel or bream zone.

The diversity of European freshwater formations is influenced not only by whether they contain stagnant (e.g. lakes, ponds, pools, creeks, etc) or flowing water (brooks, streams, rivulets, rivers), but also by their geographical position. For example, the fish fauna of northern Europe differs markedly from that of southern Europe. There are also pronounced differences between species found in the basins of the various river systems which feed the different

European seas, i.e. rivers emptying into the North Sea, the Baltic, the Mediterranean, the Black Sea and the Caspian Sea. Endemic species—fishes occurring only in a well-defined and relatively small area—form a group of their own. The best known examples are found in alpine and arctic lakes. However, endemic species also occur in relict territories like the Lake Ohrid region in Yugoslavia, which has been cut off from nearby waters since the Tertiary Era, the waters of the Iberian peninsula and Italy, and the Dalmatian rivers flowing into the Adriatic. In all these cases, the distinctive development of their fish populations was due to long-term geographical isolation under differing environmental conditions.

Reproduction

Almost all the native freshwater fishes of Europe reproduce in a similar manner. The female expels the eggs, attaching them to aquatic plants, stones or the bed, and the male then discharges milt to fertilize them. However, the Mosquito Fish (*Gambusia affinis*), originally an inhabitant of the southern part of North America, but now established in Europe, is an exception. In this species the eggs are fertilized and develop in the female's body and the young are born fully formed. This phenomenon is known as ovoviviparity.

Fish can be classified into several groups according to the substrate upon which they lay their eggs. The first, which is also the largest and the most widespread group, comprises species which spawn among aquatic plants or in meadows during spring floods and attach their eggs firmly to the plants. They are known as *phytophilous* species and include most European cyprinid fishes, together with Weatherfish, Pike and many other fishes. Lake-dwelling species in this group spawn among the bare roots of aquatic plants, the finer roots of trees growing on overhanging banks, or submerged branches.

Cyclostomes and true fishes which spawn on submerged stones or on a gravelly or sandy bed form another group. These are known as *lithophilous* and *psammophilous* species respectively, and they include the Nase, Asp, Chub, Dace, Barbel and Common Sturgeon. This group further comprises fish which spawn on the bed in special spawning-grounds or *'redds'*, such as lampreys, Salmon, Brown Trout and Grayling. These species excavate shallow depressions in the bed by means of their body and fins (lampreys also by means of their oral suckers); they then attach the fertilized eggs to stones, sand and gravel and cover them with the same material to prevent them from being washed away or discovered by predators.

The eggs of some species are pelagic; that is to say, when fertilized they float freely in a column of water until the fry hatch. One such European species is the Ziege (*Pelecus cultratus*), a curious, flat-sided cyprinid fish inhabiting the Danube, the lower reaches of its tributaries and a number of rivers flowing into the Baltic.

In the animal kingdom it is a general rule that animals which do not show parental care for their offspring, or do not conceal their eggs, usually produce far more eggs than those which do. Fish are no exception to this rule; species which lay vast quantities of eggs, such as the Pond Carp, the Pike, the Tench and the Burbot (which lays up to a million eggs), pay no further attention to their offspring. Although the survival rate is minimal and most of the young fish never attain adulthood, it is most unlikely that the entire brood would perish. Conversely, species which lay few eggs, like sticklebacks, the Bitterling, Grayling and salmonids, make some kind of provision for their offspring. Salmonids therefore prepare a redd, the Bitterling lays its eggs in the gill cavity of molluscs and sticklebacks and Mudminnows build nests made of plant material and stand guard over the eggs, often protecting the newly hatched young as well.

Most fishes live in places with an ample supply of substrate for them to spawn on, but some live in water where conditions are just not suitable. In that case they often have to wander far afield to find a suitable spot. The Nase, the East European Bream, the Ziege and many other species undertake short journeys in the breeding season, while Eels, Salmon and Sea Trout are famed for the length of their migrations.

The European Eel is a fascinating creature and has an extraordinary life-history. After spending an average of 12—15 years in fresh water, the Eels migrate downstream to the sea (i.e. they are catadromous fish). They then travel in deep water to the subtropical parts of the Atlantic Ocean, and in particular to the 'Sargasso Sea' between the Bermudas and the Bahamas, where the adult fish spawn and then die. The newly hatched larvae, which are transparent and look like willow leaves, bear no resemblance whatsoever to the adult Eels and were long thought to be a separate species; they were named *Leptocephalus brevirostris* and the larvae are still known as leptocephali.

Carried by the warm Gulf Stream, the larvae slowly swim in the direction of Europe, a journey which takes them three whole years. Once they have reached the European coast, however, the transparent leptocephali are transformed to pigmented elvers, which begin to grow and are capable of swimming actively against river currents. The Eels then attempt to migrate up most European rivers. However, damming projects and industrial and urban pollution of the water have put an end to their journeys up many big European rivers once and for all. Consequently, Eel populations in the higher reaches of some of these rivers depend entirely on the regular importation of young eels.

Today it may sound ridiculous, but it is not so very long ago that big European rivers like the Rhine and the Elbe were a veritable paradise for the kingly Salmon (*Salmo salar*). Up to the 1930's, Salmon still migrated far up the Rhine, the Elbe, the Seine, the Weser and the rivers flowing into the Baltic, against the current, to spawn in their upper reaches and those of their tributaries. The Salmon is a typical anadromous fish; that is to say, it spends most of its life in the sea and enters fresh water to spawn. Migrating male Salmon turn dark, reddish spots appear on their sides, their belly acquires a pinkish blush and their lower jaw becomes hooked; the females remain silvery grey. When migrating upstream the great fish overcome powerful currents, rapids, weirs and other low obstacles. Their spawning grounds are in the upper reaches of the rivers, in clean water with plenty of oxygen. The females excavate long depressions (redds) measuring about 3 m in a sandy or gravelly bed and in these deposit the eggs, which are then fertilized by the males. Since Salmon go without food while migrating, many of them die of exhaustion after spawning. The young Salmon (alevins) remain two or three years in the river and only then, with their parents, migrate downstream to the sea, where they spend several years growing very quickly. Spawning takes place twice or three times, although some adult Salmon have been known to migrate to fresh water to spawn every year for five years. In fresh water young Salmon live mainly on tiny invertebrate animals and small fish whereas in the sea they live entirely on fish.

On their journey upstream from the sea, Salmon are guided by the chemistry of the water. For them, every river has its own particular flavour and smell and they always swim unerringly to the place where they were born to spawn.

Other migratory fishes which have suffered the same fate as the Salmon in most big European rivers include the Sea Trout (*Salmo trutta trutta*), the Allis Shad (*Alosa alosa*) and the Common Sturgeon (*Acipenser sturio*). Human activities resulting in river pollution have also led, in many places, to disappearance of the largest cyclostome, the Sea Lamprey (*Petromyzon marinus*), and its smaller relative the Lampern (*Lampetra fluviatilis*).

Care of the offspring

As already stated above, for most European freshwater fishes the care of the future generation ends with spawning. However, there are a few species which actively look after their offspring and it is interesting to note that this is usually done by the male and seldom by the female.

The male Wels (*Silurus glanis*), for example, is a very conscientious father. After the female has deposited the eggs in a nest of aquatic plants, roots and floating brushwood, he fertilizes them and then remains on guard. If a Perch, a Pike-perch or some other predator comes along, the anxious father immediately drives it away. Furthermore, after the young hatch, the male continues to look after them until they disperse and swim away. The distantly related American Catfish, or Horned Pout (*Ictalurus nebulosus*), which has been bred in many European rivers and ponds since the end of the last century, looks after its eggs in a similar manner.

The males of two other North American fishes now established in European ponds and open water likewise take care of the eggs; these are the Large-mouth Bass (*Micropterus salmoides*) and the Pumpkin-seed Sunfish (*Lepomis gibbosus*). The former spawns in May and June in shallow water near the edge. The female lays the 10,000—15,000 eggs in a large dish-like nest some 60—80 cm in diameter prepared beforehand in the bed. The male then fertilizes them, stands guard over them, keeps them free of mud and drives away all other fish, including the female that produced them. When the young are hatched, 14 days later, the male continues to look after them and for some days takes them with him wherever he goes.

The related Pumpkin-seed Sunfish builds smaller nests, only 20—30 cm in diameter, in shallow water near the margin of stagnant or gently flowing water. Pike-perch (*Stizostedion lucioperca*) prepare large, untidy nests about 50 cm in diameter for their brood. In shallow water near the edge, they dig a depression several centimetres deep. In doing so they uncover a tangle of roots of aquatic plants, to which the female attaches the eggs, which may number well over half a million. After fertilizing the eggs the male keeps watch over them, fanning them all the time with its pectoral and ventral fins to ensure that they are constantly supplied with oxygenated water and are kept clear of fine mud. While standing guard, the male shows true devotion to duty, going without food for the entire period.

The male Moderlieschen (*Leucaspius delineatus*) and the males of both European bullheads (*Cottus gobio, C. poecilopus*), also protect their offspring conscientiously. The males of the freshwater form of the Three-spined Stickleback (*Gasterosteus aculeatus*), are famed for their vigilant care of the brood. They build nests of rootlets and grasses, in which the male keeps watch over the eggs and the fry until their yolk sacs have been absorbed and the young swim away into the surrounding water.

The way in which the Bitterling (*Rhodeus sericeus*) provides for its offspring is truly remarkable. At spawning time the males are beautifully coloured, with gleaming blue-violet sides, streaks and a posteriorly widening, opalescent blue-green stripe on the rear half of their body; their dorsal and anal fins are fiery red. The female is always silvery, but at spawning time a long, pink ovipositor appears behind her anal orifice. In the breeding season the males hunt for Swan Mussels and Freshwater Pearl Mussels on the bed of ponds and pools. When one has been chosen, the male swims hither and thither above it, chasing other males away. If a female ready for spawning comes along, however, the male circles round her with quivering movements and the two fish slowly approach the mussel. After a thorough inspection, the female comes to a halt above it and, with her head sloping downwards, releases an egg into the ovipositor. The ovipositor stiffens and straightens out and at that instant the fish thrusts the tip into the exhalant siphon of the mussel until it reaches the gill chamber. The female then expels one or two eggs, which attach themselves to the mussel's gill lamellae; the ovipositor immediately becomes limp again and the female withdraws it and swims away. Now comes the turn of the male. Quivering and jerking, he releases the milt just above the mussel's shell and the cloudy mass is drawn inside the inhalant siphon together with water. The milt thus reaches the gills from the opposite direction and fertilizes the eggs. Since bitterlings spawn several times in the course of the summer, it is not uncommon to find a whole series of eggs at different stages of development in a single mussel shell. The eggs are perfectly safe inside the shell and the fry even remain there for a short time after hatching. Although the hiding-place of the Bitterling's not very numerous offspring is a somewhat curious one, it has the virtue of being exceptionally secure. The larval fish leave the shell via the excretory siphon about 14 days after hatching, when the yolk sac is almost absorbed and they are ready to fend for themselves.

In all the species decribed above it is the male that protects the eggs and the fry. In the case of the Mudminnow, however, it is the female that looks after the young generation. This tiny fish lives in the Danubian system, in both shallow and deep water with dense aquatic vegetation, and spawns in April. On the river bed, the females build special nests which are miniature replicas of those of the Largemouth Bass, the Pumpkinseed Sunfish or the Pike-perch. The female clears away the mud round an aquatic plant until only clean sand is visible. She does this by rotating her fins, wriggling her body and pushing the mud away with her belly; the work sometimes takes two whole days. While at work the female Mudminnow is most aggressive and drives away intruders far larger than herself. When the nest is ready, the fish hovers above it and fans it with her fins; only then is she ready to spawn. For a time she loses her aggression and the patiently waiting males immediately seize the opportunity. One of them swims right up to the female and, with their bodies pressed together above the nest, the two fish begin to quiver and spawning takes place.

When the Mudminnows have finished spawning, the male loses his brilliant colours, while the female grows darker and becomes aggressive again. They keep watch over the nest and eggs, swim about incessantly above it and fan it constantly with quick movements of their pectoral fins to prevent mud from settling on it. They keep this up for about ten days, when the young fish begin to emerge from the eggs.

The River Blenny (*Blennius fluviatilis*), the only freshwater member of the blenny family in European waters, is another fish which looks after its eggs, which are hidden in spaces between stones. This bizarre little fish, which wears a kind of helmet, occurs in the south of Spain, in southern France, on many of the Mediterranean islands, in Italy, in Dalmatia, in the basin of the river Vardar and in Lake Dojran in the south-east of Macedonia. While the embryos are developing in the eggs, the male does not leave them and will even defend them against man, as well as against other fish; if anyone stretches out a hand towards its nest, it will be attacked time and time again.

The fry

Fish eggs are spherical and each is wrapped in a strong semipermeable membrane which allows water and solutes to enter the egg and permits gaseous exchange between the egg and the water. Some eggs, e.g. Carp and Pike, have a sticky surface to give them a firm hold on plants and submerged branches and stones. The size of the eggs varies with the species and is partly related to the number which the species produces. For instance, trout have comparatively few eggs up to 5 mm across, while cyprinid fish usually have a large number of eggs only 1—2 mm in diameter.

The tiny newly hatched fry bear no resemblance to the adult fish. They are generally glassily transparent and attached to their belly they have a large yolk sac which keeps them supplied with food for the first few days or weeks of life. On their head they often have cement glands enabling them to cling to aquatic plants and other objects in the water. When the yolk sac has been all but absorbed (a process which may take anything from a few days to two or three weeks or even longer), the tiny fish begins to swim about in search of food. At first it lives on the minutest morsels — the smallest planktonic organisms such as infusorians, rotifers, young developmental stages of copepods (*Cyclops*) and daphnids, and the earliest larvae of aquatic insects.

By the time the yolk sac has been completely absorbed, the little fish begins to look more like the adult animal. The pectoral fins are the first to develop; the unpaired fins are not yet present and, instead, there is a continuous fin border all the way round the body. In a few days this begins to break up into separate unpaired fins and the ventral fins make their appearance. The mouth then opens properly, the intestine develops and the swim-bladder dilates. The body gradually becomes pigmented and the first fin rays and first scales begin to be formed. Subsequently, the young fish eat vast amounts of food and grow at a brisk rate. In some species they attain sexual maturity at the end of their first or second year (e.g. the Mudminnow and the Moderlieschen), but generally this occurs in later years. The males usually mature a little sooner than the females.

Their small size and helplessness make the fry easy prey for all their numerous enemies. Chief among these are the predatory larvae of aquatic insects and many other invertebrates, but the young are also hunted by older fish and even by their own parents. The greatest enemies of the embryos of cyprinid fishes include the fry of predatory fishes, which usually hatch a few weeks earlier and are relatively large by the time the cyprinids lay their eggs. To ensure that at least some of the small fish survive the first days of their life, vast numbers of eggs are produced.

In the larval state, some fish are so different in appearance from the adult form that they were long regarded as separate species. The Eel has already been mentioned. The newly hatched Wels embryo looks surprisingly like a tadpole and the typical catfish 'whiskers' (barbels) do not appear on its head for 9—10 days. Lamprey larvae likewise differ markedly from their parents. True, they have a serpentine body, but they lack the typical oral sucker and they are blind. Their habits are also different from those of adult lampreys; they hide away in sandy or muddy creeks, brooks and rivers and live on organic débris and diatoms, whereas adult lampreys are mostly parasites and swim freely in the water.

Although not strictly freshwater creatures, flatfishes are fascinating and develop in a most remarkable manner. At the end of the 19th and the beginning of the 20th century, the Flounder (*Platichthys flesus*) still occasionally left the sea for the big European rivers and, together with salmon, sea trout, sturgeon, lampreys and other migratory species, made its way deep inland. Like the young of other fishes, flatfishes are bilaterally symmetrical at hatching. They have a relatively high body, a long fin border and a large yolk sac and their eyes, like those of other fishes, are situated on either side of their head. Within a few weeks, however, their life and appearance begins to undergo a radical change. The fish turn over on one side, leave the upper layers of the water and sink to the bottom, where they spend the rest of their life. At the same time their form alters. The once symmetrical skull becomes asymmetrical, while one of their eyes shifts to the free side of their head, which thus definitively becomes the upper side. The whole of this side of the body is dark, while the eyeless side is white.

During the first few days of life, the tiny fry of many species spend their time in warm shallow water near the edge, where they can find sufficient food (small animals) and are in less danger of being attacked by larger predatory fish. Small fry of this type almost always gather in huge shoals on the principle that there is safety in numbers.

Very often, the fry of predatory fishes display signs of cannibalism. The Pike in particular is so voracious that it will actually seize an only slightly smaller sibling. It sometimes takes several days before large prey can be swallowed and to avoid suffocation the Pike increases the supply of water to its gills by frantically opening and closing its opercula. Sometimes, however, the fish pays a high price for its greed and we not infrequently come across a Pike choked to death by a half-swallowed relative. Similar cases can also be observed (though less often) among Trout and Pike-perch.

In catches of fish we sometimes encounter specimens showing characters of two different species, such as Pond Carp × Crucian Carp, Chub × Asp, Dace × Nase, Roach × Bleak, Rudd × Silver Bream, Roach × Silver Bream and Roach × Common Bream hybrids—all within the carp family (Cyprinidae). We may also find hybrids resulting from crosses between species of different families or even orders, e.g. of a Roach (a fish belonging to the order Cypriniformes) with a Ruffe (a member of the perch family).

Hybrids occur where fish of different species spawn in the same place at the same time and the eggs of one species are fertilized by the milt of another. Such hybrids are sometimes fertile and sometimes not, but the reason is still unknown. It is likewise not clear why the eggs of one species can be fertilized by the milt of another, and yet not *vice versa*. Interspecies crossing probably played a role in the development of some endemic forms, and in other vertebrate classes as well as among fishes.

Nutrition

Most European freshwater fishes are carnivorous to one degree or another, catching a wide variety of prey including other fish. However, their commonest food-items are invertebrate animals living on the bottom or in open water, such as insect larvae, molluscs and small planktonic crustaceans.

Carp, Barbel and Bream are typical benthophages, i.e. fish which feed on small bottom-dwelling animals. Very often, and especially on warm summer days, we can see whole shoals of carp swimming slowly and quietly just below the surface, as if they were sunning themselves. Actually, they are 'grazing' plankton—small aquatic crustaceans and other organisms floating in the water. When they breathe, the fish filter these tiny creatures off, so that they remain clinging, as if caught on a mesh, to their gill-rakers, which form a dense covering on the outer surface of the gill arches.

Many European fishes live on plankton. Those which live on nothing else (e.g. many whitefishes) have long, thick gill-rakers forming an extremely fine network on which even the minutest aquatic organisms are caught. In some species we find that populations living in water with a poor supply of larger food-items have adapted to feed on plankton. An example of this are the small perch living in the Mondsee (Moon Lake) in the Austrian Alps, which have much longer gill-rakers than normal populations elsewhere and live mainly on lake plankton.

Some fish have a liking for insects which have fallen on to the water. This can best be observed in trout streams and rivers in the mountains, since when mayflies or caddis-flies swarm, trout and grayling are interested in nothing else. The Chub, Ide, Dace, Bleak and Asp also hunt insects, but each in its own way—some fish gather insects floating on the surface so cautiously that they hardly make a ripple, while others make a noise. Grayling, Dace and Bleak usually drag their prey down and devour it under water afterwards, Chub and Ide catch swimming insects by suction and Asp and Trout greedily snap them up, often leaping out of the water to do so.

Large predators have a variety of feeding techniques. The Pike lurks motionless in aquatic vegetation, under a floating uprooted tree, or in deep shadow beside the bank or a boat, and the only thing that betrays the explosive energy cooped up in its long, powerful body are the faint undulations of its pectoral fins. If a shoal of smaller fish approaches, the Pike turns almost imperceptibly, following their passage so as not to lose sight of them, and then strikes like lightning. Just before reaching its prey, the Pike opens its huge toothed jaws to their full extent, drawing in the prey with the rush of water. The Pike usually seizes the fish across its body and seldom head first. At first it stays still for a few moments but then it begins to crush its prey. As soon as the smaller fish has stopped thrashing about, the pike straightens it out and with a few quick bites and barely perceptible jerks of its head, it turns its prey round so that the head is pointing into its gullet. Of course, if the victim is very small, it is engulfed immediately after the attack.

The Pike is a solitary hunter, but some other European freshwater predators hunt in company. Pike-perch and Perch—especially when young—often pursue prey *en masse*, attacking from deep water like a kind of strike force.

The Asp (*Aspius aspius*) is a ferocious hunter of small fish. It catches them in the upper layers of the water, and consequently Bleak, Rudd and Roach are its commonest prey. The Asp attacks a shoal of such fish like a shot from a gun, making a tremendous splash. The Danube Salmon, the king of the mountain and submontane tributaries of the Danube, is even fiercer. It prefers large fish, which it often pursues so wildly that the water heaves and froths as if there were a storm. Grayling and silvery Nase are its favourite prey. The Wels is another noisy hunter. Although it normally frequents deep water, at night it often rises to the upper layers of the water in search of food.

Some European fish populations are completely herbivorous, for example adult Rudd (a common river and pond fish) which occur in pools in the Elbe basin in Bohemia. Although very young Rudds eat both plant and animal plankton, after they exceed about 7 cm in this particular site they become almost exclusively vegetarian and live on duckweed, pondweed and other soft aquatic plants. The Carp, Chub, Roach and East European Bream also like to nibble aquatic plants from time to time. In mountain streams in the Danube region, we can frequently observe whole shoals of gleaming silver Nase scraping away algae and small animals from submerged stones with their sharp-edged lips.

The Grass Carp (*Ctenopharyngodon idella*), which was imported comparatively recently into central and western Europe, is a well known herbivorous fish. It originally came from China and the Amur basin in the USSR. It is kept experimentally in a great many ponds, where it is fed on clover, lucerne and other fodder plants, but frequently escapes from them into open water. Its Far Eastern cousin, the Silver Carp (*Hypophthalmichthys molitrix*), lives on algae and is also sometimes introduced into ponds and reservoirs.

Diseases

Like dry-land animals, fish are subject to various diseases. Where they are bred intensively in ponds, regular and painstaking health monitoring of the population is essential.

Contagious diseases caused by different pathogenic organisms are the most dangerous; many of them are transmitted from one fish to another via the water, so that a great many fish are affected in a very short time. Infectious diseases are caused by a wide variety of viruses, bacteria and fungi, while the causative agents of so called invasive diseases come from the animal kingdom, the commonest being protozoans, worms and arthropods.

The most dreaded virus disease of fish is spring virus of carp (SVC), an acute form of infectious dropsy caused by *Rhabdovirus carpio*, which specifically attacks the most widespread pond-bred fish, the Pond Carp. In the spring (in April and May), it chiefly attacks young stock aged 1—2 years, weighing 300—500 g. In addition to being spread by the water in which the fish live, this dangerous viral disease is also transmitted by the sexual products during artificial spawning and by infected fishing equipment (landing nets, tanks, etc). Furthermore, the virus can survive for long periods in the mud at the bottom of an emptied pond. At water temperatures of over 10 °C it quickly multiplies, penetrates the fish's gills and attacks sundry organs, producing severe inflammation. The disease reaches its climax at temperatures of about 17 °C, when the fish die *en masse*. Diseased fish collect near the bank. Characteristically they have somewhat protruding eyes, a slightly swollen belly and minute blood spots on their skin and gills; hyperaemia and herniation of the anus are also frequent.

In regions with a high incidence of infectious dropsy the fish have to be treated with a special vaccine; in addition, an antibiotic is added to their food. Emptied reservoirs must be disinfected with large doses of quicklime (25 kg per hectare); the bed of large ponds must be thoroughly dried and places which are still contaminated disinfected with quicklime.

Similar viral infections, which are often manifested externally in extensive inflammation of the skin, necrosis and skin tumours, also occur in salmonids, eels and pike, etc.

Fish furunculosis is a common bacterial disease among salmonid fishes. It is caused by *Aeromonas salmonicida*, rod-shaped bacteria which first attack the intestine but ultimately produce deep furuncular ulcers in the muscles, so that the fish eventually die. *A. punctata*, a related microorganism, causes chronic infectious dropsy of carp in warm spring and summer weather; the infection is likewise manifested in the appearance of deep ulcers in the skin. The best way of treating bacterial diseases is to administer antibiotics in granulated food or to inject them. It also helps to bathe the fish in antibiotic solutions.

Fungal diseases include branchiomycosis, a fungal infection of the gills caused by *Branchiomyces sanguinis*, which leads to occlusion of the blood vessels and eventually to death. This disease has been found in Pike, Rainbow Trout, whitefishes and catfish, as well as in various cyprinid fishes (Carp, Tench, Crucian Carp). It occurs in the summer, i.e. when it is warm, in over-populated and organically contaminated water. As soon as the first signs make their appearance, the water must be disinfected with quicklime and subsequently continuously checked to see that it remains clean.

Injuries (e.g. by ice) are frequently followed by saprolegniosis, in which the mycelium of a certain kind of mould grows out of the wound and rapidly spreads, forming shaggy, whitish grey patches on the body. Any fish can be attacked, especially in the winter and the spring. Affected fish should be given long baths in malachite green solution (0.2—0.5 mg/l water over a period of three to four days).

Trypanosomoses and trypanoplasmoses are invasive diseases caused by protozoans (blood flagellates belonging to the genera *Trypanosoma* and *Trypanoplasma*). The intermediate hosts of these flagellates are leeches, in whose alimentary tract the protozoans proliferate asexually by simple division; the young flagellates penetrate into the leeches' suctorial apparatus and are then transmitted in the saliva to the next host—a carp, tench or pike—in which their growth is completed. Sick fish are listless and emaciated and have anaemic gills; they are treated by long-term bathing in gentian violet solution. The disease can be prevented by keeping the incidence of leeches systematically down. The danger of leeches is not confined to their role as intermediate hosts of flagellates. For example, a mass incidence of the fish leech *Piscicola geometra*, which clings to carp skin, gills and fins, makes the fish very weak and is sometimes fatal.

Helminthoses—infestation by parasitic worms—are frequent among fishes. Protection is very troublesome; it involves submersion baths in solutions of various chemicals (milk of lime, formaldehyde, etc) and is more or less specific for individual parasites. Some helminthoses are at present incurable. Dangerous parasites include the gill nematodes of the family Dactylogyridae, which attach themselves to the gills, fins and skin of the most diverse fishes and, in the case of mass infestation, can cause suffocation, swelling of the gills and sometimes necrosis and death.

Infestation by tapeworms—especially if several worms attack one fish—can also prove fatal. The sexually mature tapeworms parasitize the fish's intestine, while larval stages may also attack other organs. Tapeworms generally have complex life-histories. The adult worms produce eggs, which are released together with the excreta of the host into the water. The larvae penetrate into the body of the first intermediate host (usually a planktonic crustacean, a threadworm or a water flea), where their development continues. They then either invade further intermediate hosts or attack the final host directly. In fish intermediate hosts, the cysts of the parasites often appear in their liver and body cavity, while fish which serve as the final host have a noticeably distended belly crammed full of tapeworms.

Arthropod parasites comprise carp lice (genus *Argulus*), parasitic copepods (e.g. *Ergasilus sieboldi*) and various other crustaceans.

During the past few decades there has been a steady increase in mass fish deaths for which man is directly responsible. Every year, poisonous industrial, agricultural and urban waste wreaks increasing havoc among fish living in rivers and streams, sometimes to the point of a real disaster.

Catching fish with net and line

Catching fish with nets in open water is much more complicated than harvesting them from a pond. One cannot empty a dam or a river and simply haul in the fish with a seine as one can in a pond, but must literally 'fish' for them. Several types of nets are used for this purpose.

The largest is a long dragnet or seine employed in lakes and dams, which is often several hundred metres long and eight, ten or more metres high and is usually drawn by a motor-boat. The dragnet generally has relatively large meshes, so that only large and older fish are caught, while small fish slip through, back into the river, lake or dam. This net is suitable only for places with a smooth bed free from any obstructions with which the bottom lead might become entangled. Such fishing is particularly successful at night, when all is quiet and the fish are concentrated in shallow water near the edge, looking for food.

Gill nets are usually 30—40 m long and 3—4 m high, with large meshes; they hang in the water, at right angles to the surface, like curtains which the fish cannot see. As the fish swim along near the bank they get caught in the net, generally by their gills, but sometimes by the front of their dorsal fin. Nowadays gill nets are made of fine fishing-line nylon or nylon fibres; they are light, but very strong, and are virtually invisible in water. The size of the meshes depends on the size of the fish the fishermen want to catch. For Roach, Perch, small whitefishes and other small fish they should measure 3 × 3 cm, while the meshes of gill nets used for catching prize catfish, carp, Pike-perch and Asp measure 10×10, 12×12 and even 15×15 cm.

Fish traps and drop-nets are often employed for fishing in rivers, dams and—particularly—lakes. Drop-nets have long 'leaders' joined to the actual trap, from which the fish are unable to escape. Shoals of fish grazing in a shallow backwater swim along inside the leaders until they come to a place where the net suddenly narrows like the neck of a funnel. After swimming through this, they emerge into a large space bounded by nets and are unable to find their way back. All the fishermen have to do is to inspect the nets several times a day and take out the catch.

Fishing with dip-nets—square nets with corners made of pliant branches or wires fixed in a tubular diagonal cross-piece—is of only minor importance on large lakes, where it is successful chiefly in the spawning season. Small dip-nets 1 m square, with approximately 1 cm meshes, are employed by anglers to catch fish bait.

Angling is one of man's oldest economic activities. Evidence that prehistoric European hunters already caught fish 1,000—2,000 years B.C. is furnished by finds in palafittes, where various bone fishing implements—the first step towards modern angling—have been discovered.

Angling is still an important recreational pursuit and has some economic value as well. Not only does it provide welcome additions to the dinner table but it also gives us a greater knowledge, love and understanding of nature. It thus contributes to our overall fulfilment in a hi-tec society so devoid of relaxing pastimes.

Fishermen who are responsible for fishing in open water should watch the numbers and health of the fish in their area, see that the water is kept well stocked and keep an account of the number of fish caught by anglers. Fish populations in open water can be safeguarded by careful planning and by keeping good records. Anglers should be concerned with the number and species of introduced fish, the number of

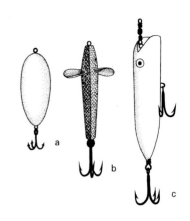

Spoon lure (a), Devon (b) and wobbler (c)

angling licences in the individual areas and the close season for individual species. Also of importance is the daily permissible number of fish that can be caught by anglers, the minimum permissible size of fish to be removed and the technique by which the fish can be caught.

For angling we can use natural or artificial bait. Natural bait (a worm, a grasshopper, a potato, a piece of dough, a small fish) is employed for four different basic types of angling—float-fishing, bottom-fishing, spinning and fly-fishing.

In float-fishing the bait floats either on the water surface, or at different depths in the water column above the bed. In bottom-fishing, the bait lies on the bed, sometimes unweighted and sometimes held down by a lead weight. Predatory fish are normally caught by spinning. The bait, a dead fish, a spoon lure or a Devon, is generally kept about half-way down the water column (in shallow mountain rivers just below the surface). The most skilful art, however, is fly-fishing, which requires very fine, light fishing tackle, patience as a learner and years of practice. Various real insects (stone-flies, grasshoppers, may-

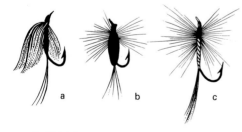

Artificial flies: a — wet, b, c — dry

Swivel

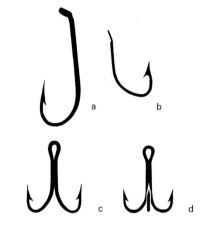

Types of hooks: a — single hook with loop, b — single hook with blade, c — double hook, d — triple hook

flies) or artificial flies (dry, i.e. floating on the surface, or wet, i.e. submerged) are employed as bait.

The rod is an extension of the angler's right arm. He casts the bait with it, it tells him when a fish takes a nibble and he hooks, plays and finally hauls the fish in with it. Since different fishes are caught by different techniques—trout and Grayling with flies, Pike and Pike-perch by spinning and carp by float-fishing or on the bottom—the corresponding rods are also different.

The reel is another important part of the modern angler's tackle. Fly-fishing requires light, simple reels with about 50 m of standard line and 30 m of thicker line. For spinning and other types of angling we nowadays use fixed spoon reels or multiplier reels. Almost all lines are now made of nylon, which is

smooth, almost invisible in water, flexible and exceedingly strong. Big predators are angled with a stranded steel wire line, which should be fitted with swivels to prevent it from becoming twisted.

Lead weights are used to keep the bait in a specific place or at a specific depth. When trolling with a dead fish in a strong current, a lead cap is attached to its head.

The fish-hook, to which we fasten the bait and with which we actually catch the fish, is sharply barbed. Hooks with a double barb are used for angling predators with a live fish bait; triple barbs are fitted onto spinners and spoons for angling with dead bait.

Many forms of angling require floats to keep the bait at a fixed depth and to signal a nibble. Here again we distinguish several types—virtually one for every type of angling. The simplest are made of goose quills, the modern equivalents being made of celluloid and plastic. Floats with a large, round or elongate cork are used for angling with a live fish bait. For float-fishing in deep

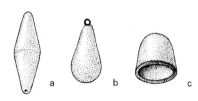

Types of lead weights: a — running, b — terminal, c — cap, head weight

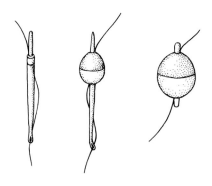

Floats

water we use sliding floats with a hole allowing the line to pass freely through it; a small stopper is then attached to the line at the required distance from the bait.

Another important item is the landing net for lifting the fish out of the water; a folding net is very practical. Large fish are sometimes landed with a gaff.

Anglers also need a net in which the fish they have caught can be kept in water until it is time to go home. Nowadays the relevant shops offer a wide range of mechanical and electrical devices which are supposed to tell the angler when a fish bites or even when to hook it. Such devices have nothing to do with real angling; they take all the poetry and spirit out of it and merely impoverish it—something that no true angler would ever want.

Days spent in angling are full of experiences, poetry and pleasure. Every angler looks forward to the day when he will catch his big fish, but is not put out if he fails to do so. There is still tomorrow, next week, next year . . . Sitting beside the river, which is always the same and yet always changing, we begin to see life and the world quite differently from the way they appear to us in the every day rush; we see them as an inseparable whole of which we ourselves are a tiny part. Angling teaches us humility. It also gives us a better understanding of the world around us and of ourselves, and that is perhaps what modern man, in this hi-tec world, needs more than anything else.

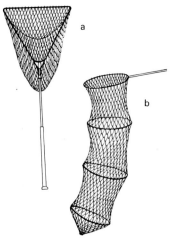

Landing net (a) and holding net (b)

The systematic position of bony fishes and cyclostomes within the animal kingdom

Kingdom: Animalia

Phylum: Chordata. Animals which at some time in their lives have a nerve cord.
            Chordata are then divided into subphyla.

Sub-phylum: 1. Hemichordata
            2. Cephalochordata
            3. Urochordata
            4. Vertebrata. Animals with developed vertebrae to one degree or another, and a nerve cord with a developed anterior end housed in a cranium.
            Vertebrata are then divided into 2 superclasses.

Superclass 1: Agnatha

    Class: Cyclostomata. Vertebrates with no proper jaws, e.g. Lampreys.

Superclass 2: Gnathostomata. Vertebrates with jaws. Divided into the following classes:

    Class: Elasmobranchii. Fishes with a basically cartilaginous skeleton, e.g. sharks and rays. No European freshwater representatives.

    Class: Osteichthyes. Fishes with a basically bony skeleton. All European freshwater jawed fishes belong to this Class. Divided into 13 or so Orders in Europe, the most primitive of which is the Order Chondrostei containing the sturgeons.

    Class: Amphibia

    Class: Reptilia

    Class: Aves

    Class: Mammalia

Classification and identification of European freshwater fishes

As mentioned in the introduction, there are about two hundred species of freshwater cyclostomes and bony, true fishes in European rivers and lakes.

Lampreys—members of the primitive class of cyclostomes—are jawless aquatic vertebrates (Superclass Agnatha). Some of their approximately ten European representatives are anadromous migratory species, such as the Sea Lamprey (*Petromyzon marinus*) and the Lampern (*Lampetra fluviatilis*), while others live only in fresh water, like the Brook Lamprey (*L. planeri*) and the Danube Lamprey (*L. danfordi*). They differ as regards their size and form and the position of their dorsal fins, but the main characteristic feature of each species is its dentition. Lamprey larvae do not have an oral sucker like the adults and their small mouth, with its fleshy lips, is adapted for the intake of minute food particles (organic débris and algae). The Sea Lamprey grows to a length of over 1 m, but some resident freshwater species measure no more than 15 cm.

All European freshwater true fishes belong to the superclass Gnathostomata and the class Osteichthyes. Their body is clearly divided into three parts—a head, a trunk and a tail and they have a basically bony skeleton and well developed jaws.

To be able to determine the various genera and species exactly, we need to know a fish's most important characters. One of them is the position of the mouth, i.e. whether it is at the end of the snout (a terminal mouth), on the upper surface of the snout (a superior or dorsal mouth), or on the under side (an inferior or ventral mouth).

Useful identification features are found on the gills. The gills are protected by movable covers known as opercula; these are composed of four flat opercular bones whose reciprocal position and shape in some fishes (e.g. salmonids) are species specific. Beneath the opercula are found the red gills on four branchial arches; on the inner surface of the branchial arches are the gill-rakers, the number of which on the first branchial arch is also important for the identification of many fishes. In cyprinid fishes the fifth branchial arch has been converted to two pharyngeal bones with one, two or three rows of pharyngeal teeth; the number and shape of these

Fish mouths: a — superior or dorsal,
b — terminal, c — inferior or ventral

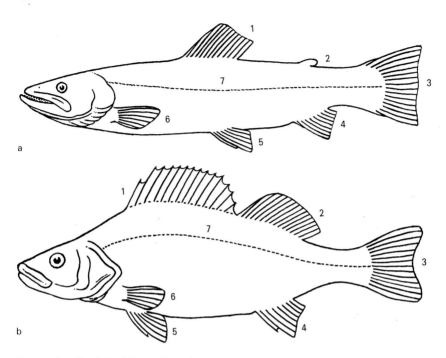

Topography of a fish: a) Brown Trout (1 — dorsal fin, 2 — adipose fin, 3 — caudal fin, 4 — anal fin, 5 — ventral fins, 6 — pectoral fins, 7 — lateral line); b) Perch (1 — first dorsal fin, 2 — second dorsal fin, 3 — caudal fin, 4 — anal fin, 5 — ventral fins, 6 — pectoral fins, 7 — lateral line)

teeth likewise helps in the exact determination of members of this family.

The organization of the teeth on the vomer (one of the bones reinforcing the under side of the skull) and the shape of the vomer are useful identification features in salmonid fishes.

A further basic identification feature of fish is the position and shape of the fins and the number of hard and soft rays in them. The relative positions of the dorsal and ventral fins, the shape of the caudal fin and the relative positions of the ventral and pectoral fins are all important. One of the distinguishing characters of salmonids, whitefishes and the American Catfish is the small adipose fin on the back, behind the dor-

sal fin. Equally important are the scales (especially their number in the lateral line). A further identification feature is the sharp ridge which forms a keel on the under side of the body in front of the anal orifice; in some species the keel is bare, in some it is covered with scales and in others it is absent, so that here the belly is rounded.

The basic systematic unit of all animals, including cyclostomes and bony fishes, is the species. Very often, within its geographical range a species evolves into a number of geographically isolated forms related by a series of intermediate characters; these forms are known as subspecies or geographical races. The subspecies from which the species was described is termed the nominate form and the third word in its name is the same as the second (e.g. *Salmo trutta trutta*). In other subspecies, the third word differs from the second. Small differences may also be present within the range of a subspecies, in which case we call them varieties. In addition, there are other forms dependent not on geographical, but on ecological conditions (the depth and temperature of the water, the food supply, etc); these are known as morphs. A hereditary colour difference, like the one known in the Orfe or Goldfish, is termed an aberration.

Related species are grouped together in genera. The scientific name of a species consists of two words, the first of which is the name of the genus (written with a capital letter) and the other the name of the species (written with a small letter). After the specific name comes the name of the author who first described the species, sometimes together with the year. If we wish to specify that an animal belongs to a given subspecies, variety, morph or aberration, we add a third word (with a small initial letter), if necessary together with the relevant abbreviation.

The systematic unit in which the genus is grouped is the family, which comprises several interrelated genera. Related families are grouped together in an order and orders in a class. The systematic classificaton of the golden aberration of the Ide (the Orfe) would thus be as follows:

Superclass: Gnathostomata. Vertebrates with jaws.
Class: Osteichthyes. Fishes with a basically bony skeleton.
Order: Ostariophysi. Carp and allies.
Family: Cyprinidae. Carp.
Genus: *Leuciscus*.
Species: *Leuciscus idus*. Ide.
Aberration: *Leuciscus idus* aberr. *orfus*. Orfe.

In the more primitive members of the class Osteichthyes, only some parts of the skull are bony, while the rest of the skeleton is cartilaginous. These fish belong to the order Chondrostei and all the members have an asymmetrical (heterocercal) caudal fin, whose upper lobe is much longer than the lower lobe and has a very thick upper edge. In Europe they are represented by the Sturgeon family, Acipenseridae. Their other characteristic features are the five longitudinal rows of bony plates or scutes which cover their body like armour. Sturgeons generally have a long snout and barbels (tactile appendages) in front of their inferior mouth. Most of the seven sturgeon species occurring in Europe grow to a considerable size; the biggest of them is the famous Great Sturgeon or Beluga (*Huso huso*), renowned for its caviar.

All other European freshwater fishes have jaws and belong to 12 orders of fishes. Their skull and the rest of their skeleton, including the vertebrae, is completely ossified and they have a symmetrical (homocercal) caudal fin. Their skin is usually covered with scales, but is sometimes scaleless; very occasionally it may be covered with bony plates (e.g. sticklebacks).

The members of the herring family (Clupeidae) have relatively large, loose scales and no detectable lateral line on their sides. They have a scale-covered keel on their belly and frequently have an adipose membrane on their eyes. Two of the nine European members of this family occur in western Europe and the rest in the region of the Black and the Caspian Sea, where they form many subspecies; they are mostly migratory anadromous fishes.

The members of the salmon family (Salmonidae) are characterized by a small adipose fin on their back behind the dorsal fin, small scales and a relatively large, toothed mouth devoid of barbels. They have a well developed lateral line. The majority are migratory anadromous fishes, but various resident freshwater forms also exist. In Europe there are seven species (one of which was introduced here) and a large number of geographical races. Salmonids have a wide range of sizes, from fish measuring up to 150 cm to far smaller species.

Whitefishes (family Coregonidae) also have an adipose fin. They have a relatively smaller mouth than salmonids, however, and larger scales. A great many species are distributed over northern Europe, in mountain lakes in the Alpine region and in many English, Scottish, Scandinavian, North German and Polish lakes, also in lakes Ladoga and Onega. They are classified in two genera — *Coregonus* and *Leucichthys*. The various species in these two genera contain both migratory and resident populations. Their systematics are very problematical, owing to the tremendous plasticity of the individual species.

The family Osmeridae is represented in Europe by a single species, the Smelt (*Osmerus eperlanus*), a slender, transparent little fish with a large mouth and an adipose fin. It is found in river mouths along the European coast from the north of Spain to the south of Scandinavia. A separate subspecies, *O. eperlanus dentex*, lives in rivers flowing into the White Sea.

The only native European representative of the Thymallidae family is the Grayling (*Thymallus thymallus*), a prominent inhabitant of submontane rivers and streams, which is greatly prized by anglers. The related *T. arcticus baicalensis* has been introduced experimentally into some European dams. Grayling are characterized by a strikingly high and (especially in the males) brightly coloured dorsal fin, an adipose fin and greyish silvery sides.

Pike (family Esocidae) are characterized by a long, muscular body, a posteriorly situated dorsal fin and long jaws armed with teeth. Their only European representative, the Pike (*Esox lucius*), is a familiar predator.

Family Petromyzonidae

Family Acipenseridae

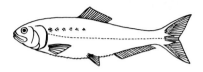

Family Clupeidae

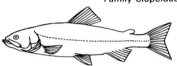

Family Salmonidae

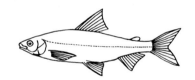

Family Coregonidae

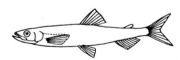

Family Osmeridae

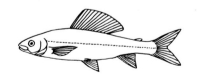

Family Thymallidae

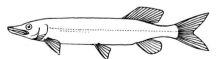

Family Esocidae

Family Umbridae

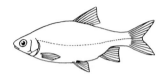

Family Cyprinidae

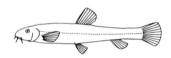

Family Cobitidae

Family Anguillidae

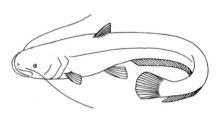

Family Siluridae

Family Ictaluridae

In the Mudminnow, the only European member of the related family Umbridae, the dorsal fin is also situated far back on the body. This small brown fish inhabits overgrown water in the middle and lower reaches of the Danube, the Prut and the Dnestr.

The members of the large carp family (family Cyprinidae) all possess Weberian ossicles, small bones connecting the vestibular apparatus in their head to their swim-bladder. The ventral fins of cyprinid fishes lie a long way behind their pectoral fins and are not reinfoced with hard, spiny rays; an adipose fin is not present. Cyprinid fishes have no teeth in their jaws, but their fifth branchial arch has been converted to pharyngeal teeth. In the spawning season, many of them develop a conspicuous spawning rash on their body, head and fins. Over 80 members of this family live in European rivers and lakes.

Loaches (family Cobitidae) are mostly small, long-bodied fish with a large number of barbels round their mouth. The largest, the Weatherfish (*Misgurnus fossilis*), has ten barbels, while the smaller loaches of the genera *Cobitis*, *Sabanejewia* and *Noemacheilus* have six. Some species have an erectile bony spine below each eye. There are 12 members of this family in Europe.

The European Eel (*Anguilla anguilla*) is the only representative of the eel family (family Anguillidae). It is characterized by a long, snake-like body and absence of the ventral fins.

One of the biggest European freshwater fishes, the European Catfish or Wels (*Silurus glanis*, family Siluridae), has a scaleless body, a wide head and a huge mouth with two long barbels on the upper jaw and four shorter ones on the lower jaw. Its North American relative, the American Catfish or Horned Pout (*Ictalurus nebulosus*, family Ictaluridae), has four barbels on each jaw and a small adipose fin behind the dorsal fin. It has been introduced into many parts of Europe.

Tooth carps (family Cyprinodontidae) are represented in Europe by two genera with three species. Their characteristic features are a flat-topped head and a superior mouth.

The Mosquito Fish (*Gambusia affinis*), the only member of the family Poeciliidae to have been imported into Europe, is an ovoviviparous species. The male's anal fin has been converted to a pairing organ (gonopodium) and the eggs are fertilized inside the female's body.

The small, slim fishes belonging to the sand smelt family (family Atherinidae) are characterized by two dorsal fins situated close together, one behind the other. The three European species inhabit the Mediterranean, the Black Sea and the Caspian Sea, but also occur in various south European lakes.

Grey mullets (family Mugilidae) have two clearly separate dorsal fins and a strikingly flattened head. They are sea fish, but quite often stray into brackish and fresh water. This family is represented by six species in fresh water in Europe.

The members of the large perch family (family Percidae) also have two dorsal fins, the first of which is reinforced with hard, sharp-pointed rays. The fish belonging to this family have rough ctenoid scales and their ventral fins are situated below their pectoral fins. Of their six genera and twelve species occurring in fresh water in Europe, the most widespread are the Perch (*Perca fluviatilis*), the Pike-perch (*Stizostedion lucioperca*) and the Ruffe (*Acerina cernua*).

Roccus labrax, the representative of the marine family Serranidae, is characterized by three hard rays in the anal fin and a relatively short and high first dorsal fin. It often strays into rivers.

The American sunfishes (family Centrarchidae) are related to the perches and two of their species have become acclimatized in European waters. To distinguish the two families you must look at their dorsal fins.

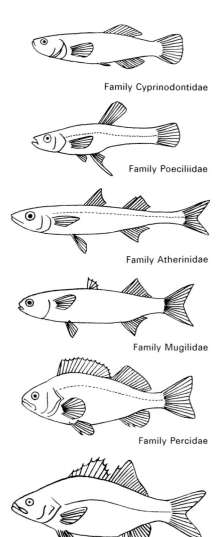

Family Cyprinodontidae

Family Poeciliidae

Family Atherinidae

Family Mugilidae

Family Percidae

Family Serranidae

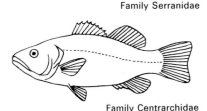

Family Centrarchidae

Family Gobiidae

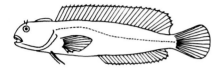

Family Blenniidae

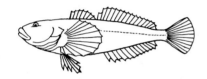

Family Cottidae

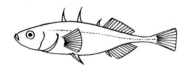

Family Gasterosteidae

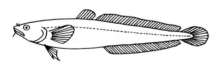

Family Gadidae

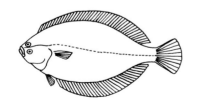

Family Pleuronectidae

The characteristic features of the twenty or so species of partly freshwater European gobies (family Gobiidae) are their ventral fins, which are fused together to form a suction disk. Most gobies are small, flat-backed benthic marine fish which often visit brackish and fresh water; some of them travel long distances up European rivers against the current, such as the Mottled Black Sea Goby (*Proterorhinus marmoratus*) which not only occurs in the Black Sea and brackish water, but is also to be found far up the Danube and its tributaries.

The River Blenny, the only freshwater representative of the blennies (family Blenniidae), has a typical 'crested' blenny head with short outgrowths above the eyes. It occurs in Mediterranean rivers and lakes.

Bullheads (family Cottidae) have a large, wide head, a large mouth and a short, spiny first dorsal fin; their scaleless body is another typical feature. Three species are to be found in fresh water in Europe.

Sticklebacks (Gasterosteidae) are remarkable for the position of their dorsal fin, which lies near the end of their body and is preceded by a few single spines. These small fish have scaleless bodies, but in some species their sides may be covered with large bony plates. There are three freshwater species in Europe.

The only European freshwater species of the large marine cod family (Gadidae) is the Burbot (*Lota lota*), which has one relatively long, fleshy barbel on its chin and two shorter barbels near its nostrils. It has two dorsal fins and a very long anal fin; its ventral fins lie anteriorly to the pectoral fins.

The last fish family occurring in European fresh waters are the flatfishes (family Pleuronectidae); these have an unmistakable flattened body, on which the eyes are situated on the dark upper side, while the pale under side is eyeless. Two species penetrate into European rivers while migrating.

Future prospects

Just as all terrestrial animals including man and terrestrial plants have evolved to live in air, fish and other aquatic organisms can live only in water. And just as clean air is of fundamental importance for organisms living on dry land, clean, well-oxygenated water is vital for the survival of fish in rivers, streams, lakes and the sea.

Man pollutes water far more than he does the air. The volume of air in which our planet is wrapped is enormous and so, except in places with an accumulation of industry or in big cities, it takes a long time for its quality to deteriorate. Human interference with water is often horrifyingly drastic, however.

From time to time we read with indignation about pollution of the sea and ecological catastrophes caused by accidents involving huge oil tankers, for example, but the situation in many European rivers, both large and small, is infinitely worse. Here we are faced not with single catastrophes, but with continuous, incessant and increasing pollution of hundreds and thousands of kilometres of rivers and the destruction of all life there, which has been going on for dozens of years. Rivers are used as sewers for poisonous industrial waste and for the incredibly vast amounts of household and other waste that come from villages, towns and cities. Furthermore, increasingly intensive crop-production means that more and more poisonous insecticides, herbicides and fertilisers seep into the ground and find their way into the water.

Progress cannot be stopped and so the consequences of advancing civilization, such as the building of factories, increased industrial production, the intensification of agriculture and the building of human settlements are all inevitable consequences of the development of our society. On the other hand, it is high time that we took active and effective steps to safeguard those things essential for our survival. In other words, we should protect our environment, of which rivers form an inseparable part.

It is not so very long ago—only in the 1930's—that Sea Trout, Salmon and Sturgeon still migrated deep into continental Europe from the North Sea via the rivers, but in most places pollution and high dams, etc, have put an end to their journeys once and for all. During the past few decades, with the tremendous development of industry, grayling, trout and various other valuable fishes have suffered a similar fate. The number of poisoned stretches of European rivers, often dozens of kilometres long, devoid of any form of life is steadily increasing.

Purification plants are undoubtedly very expensive to build, but if the waters of Europe are to remain life-giving, these plants will have to be built beside all big sources of water pollution; the money and work invested in them will be repaid with interest to all of us, since the only way in which we can lead a full and contented life is in a healthy environment—and that includes good, clean water.

Illustrations

Explanatory notes:

● — migratory species

◑ — species endangered in Europe

○ — economically important species

■ — sport fishing species

□ — introduced species

▶ — fish used as bait

▷ — marine species entering rivers

♂ — male

♀ — female

juv. — juvenile

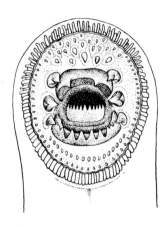

Suctorial mouth of *L. japonica*

Distribution of *L. fluviatilis*

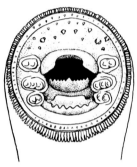

Suctorial mouth of *L. fluviatilis*

Lampern; River Lamprey
Lampetra fluviatilis (L.)

●◐
Lampreys
Petromyzonidae

The Lampern is a cyclostome vertebrate about 40 cm long, with a serpentine body and with characteristically arranged teeth in its funnel-shaped mouth. Its back and sides are dark bluish grey or greyish green and its belly is silvery white, sometimes with grey spots. The two parts of its dorsal fin meet at their base.

The Lampern lives in European coastal waters from the south of Norway to half-way down the Italian coast; in some of the big European lakes (Ladoga, Onega) a permanently freshwater form exists. In the breeding season migratory Lamperns leave the sea and migrate up European rivers to their higher reaches. On the way, they acquire a bronze tinge and stop eating, while their digestive organs degenerate and their teeth become blunt. In the sea

they are light shy, but while migrating they lose this aversion and in the upper reaches of the rivers even frequent shallow water well lit by the sun.

Just before spawning their dorsal fins grow noticeably larger and the under side of their body in front of the anal fin (the urogenital papilla) swells; in the males the papilla is produced to a spur-like structure. The male excavates a redd by wriggling its body and removes any pebbles with the aid of its mouth. It then attaches itself to the back of the female's head and wraps itself round her body in front of the first dorsal fin until their cloacae lie side by side. As the female expels the eggs, the male at once fertilizes them and with undulating movements of their body the two Lamperns immediately cover them with stirred-up sand. One mating lasts

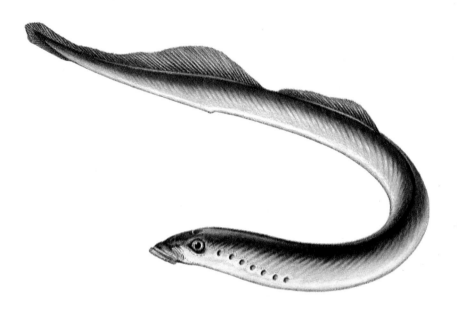

Lampetra fluviatilis

only a few seconds and the number of released eggs is small. More and more males take part, however, so that the total number of eggs from a single female amounts to 10,000 to 25,000. The adult Lamperns die soon after spawning.

The tiny larvae hatch after anything from nine to twenty days, according to the temperature. After their yolk sac has been absorbed they leave the redd and go in search of a quiet, muddy backwater. Here they spend 4—6 years buried in the sand, in tunnels whose upper wall they reinforce with a secretion from special glands situated near their gill apertures. The larvae, which are blind, have no suctorial apparatus and their mouth, armed with two fleshy lips, always protrudes a little way above the bed, facing counter to the current so as to be able to catch organic débris and microscopic algae carried along by the water. In due course they become adult Lamperns, mature and, in the spring, migrate to the sea, where they generally spend two summers before migrating upstream again to spawn. In the sea, the Lampern lives on the body fluids and flesh of small fish, to which it attaches itself by its suctorial mouth. Its oral funnel contains glands whose secretion prevents the blood of its victims from clotting.

The Lampern is of considerable economic importance, especially in the Baltic region, where it is caught in large numbers while migrating and in some places is regarded as a great delicacy.

The related Arctic Lamprey, *Lampetra japonica* (Martens), which occurs in the Bering Sea, the Sea of Okhotsk and the White Sea, is another migratory species of local economic significance.

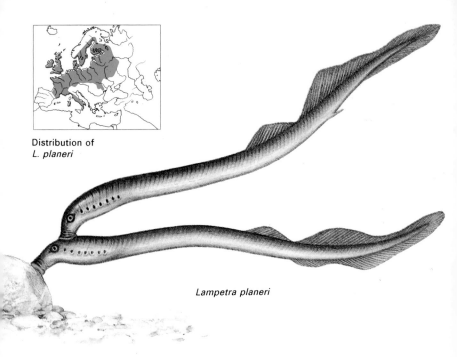

Lampetra planeri

Brook Lamprey
Lampetra planeri (Bloch)

Lampreys
Petromyzonidae

The small, non-parasitic Brook Lamprey is seldom more than 25 cm long and is a permanent freshwater resident. It differs from the related Danube Lamprey in respect of its second dorsal fin, which is in close contact with the posterior edge of the first fin. It is coloured similarly to the Lampern, but at spawning time its mouth (in both sexes) and the area round its anal orifice (in the females) turn rusty red.

The Brook Lamprey lives in small submontane and mountain rivers and streams. It occurs in the tributaries of the rivers flowing into North Sea and the Baltic and in some of the tributaries of the upper reaches of the Volga, Tisa, Morava and Drava, etc.

It spawns in the upper parts of these waters in May and June. In a sandy and pebbly bed the wriggling males and females form rounded depressions in which the female lays the eggs and the male, wrapped round its body, fertilizes them. Again, several males take part in the spawning process. The larvae spend 3—7 years in sand, clay and mud deposits in quiet water, where they live on organic débris and diatoms. During their transformation to adult lampreys they develop an oral sucker and eyes; when they attain sexual maturity their digestive organs gradually stop functioning. After their metamorphosis they spend a short time resting and then migrate upstream again to spawn. The females die 10—15 days after spawning; the males survive 20—40 days.

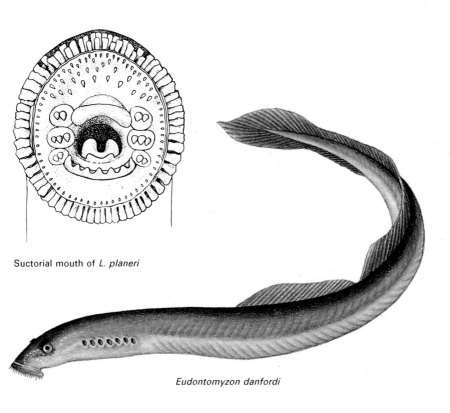

Suctorial mouth of *L. planeri*

Eudontomyzon danfordi

Danube Lamprey
Eudontomyzon danfordi REGAN

Lampreys
Petromyzonidae

This inhabitant of the Danube basin is about 25—30 cm long. Like the Brook Lamprey, it is a permanent freshwater resident found in the headwaters of the Danube and its tributaries. It differs from the Brook Lamprey in the arrangement of the teeth in its funnel-like mouth and the greater distance between its dorsal fins. After its metamorphosis it usually lives a further two or three years and adopts a parasitic mode of life; it attaches itself to fish by its sucker, scrapes a hole in their skin and sucks out the blood and flesh. As in the case of the Brook Lamprey, the full-grown larvae of the Danube Lamprey are often a little larger than the adult animals.

The somewhat smaller Ukrainian Lamprey, *Eudontomyzon mariae* Berg, found in the rivers flowing into the Baltic, the Adriatic, the Aegean, the Black Sea and the Sea of Azov, measures about 20 cm. *E. hellenicus* (Vladykov, Kott et Economidis), which occurs in the Aegean basin, is another small lamprey.

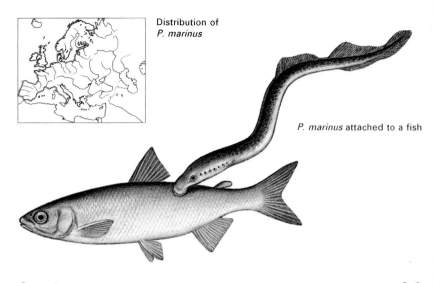

Distribution of
P. marinus

P. marinus attached to a fish

Sea Lamprey
Petromyzon marinus L.

●◑
Lampreys
Petromyzonidae

The Sea Lamprey, which can measure over 1 m and weigh up to 2 kg, is the largest European cyclostome. It has a typical oral sucker armed with many concentric rows of horny teeth of various sizes. Its back is greyish green, with dark mottling, and its belly is yellowish white. Its dorsal fin is divided distinctly into two parts, of which the posterior part is continuous with the caudal fin.

This lamprey migrates from the sea up European rivers, from the north of Scandinavia to Gibraltar and in the Mediterranean eastwards to Yugoslavia and the Albanian shores of the Adriatic. It does not occur in the Black Sea or its tributary rivers and is relatively rare in the Baltic, although it can be encountered eastwards as far as the river Neva in the USSR.

In Europe, this anadromous marine species migrates to fresh water in March and April, but does not actually spawn there until May to July of the following year. Its spawning sites usually lie at a depth of about 1 m of water in a sandy and/or stony bed. As distinct from other lampreys, Sea Lampreys spawn only in couples. With their oral sucker and with undulating movements of their body, the males form shallow redds, in which the females deposit 60,000—300,000 eggs about 1 mm in diameter. The tiny larvae, which hatch in 8—20 days (according to the temperature of the water), remain three to five years in muddy, clayey or sandy backwaters. They then undergo metamorphosis and as adult lampreys migrate downstream to the sea, where for a few more years they feed parasitically on mackerel, cod and other large fishes, to which they attach themselves by their suctorial mouth. During the lampreys' spawning migration, their digestive apparatus degenerates. Consequently, they are unable to eat and soon after spawning they die.

As in the Great Lakes of North America, the Sea Lamprey probably also has a permanent freshwater form in certain

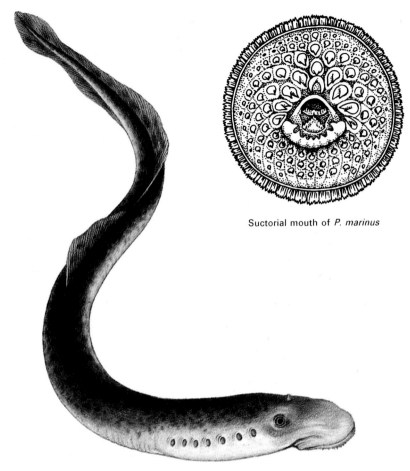

Suctorial mouth of *P. marinus*

Petromyzon marinus

European lakes. At the beginning of the twentieth century, it still regularly migrated up the big European rivers, like the Seine, the Rhine and the Elbe, to spawn; in the Rhine it was recorded as far upstream as Basle, while in the Elbe it swam against the current until it reached the Vltava and its tributaries. Today, water construction works and pollution have made migration impossible. In the past the Sea Lamprey was economically very important, but now there are only a few places where it can be caught while migrating.

The Caspian Lamprey, *Caspiomyzon wagneri* (Kessler), which measures about 50 cm and inhabits the Caspian region, resembles the Sea Lamprey, but is uniformly grey and lacks the dark mottling. From September to December it migrates from the Caspian Sea up the Volga, the Ural, the Terek and other rivers. Economically it is relatively important, but owing to water construction works undertaken on these rivers its numbers there have fallen severely in recent years.

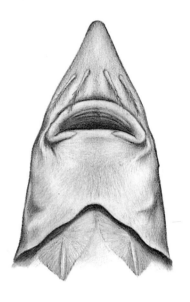

View of the underside of the head of
H. huso

Great Sturgeon; Beluga
Huso huso (L.)

●○
Sturgeon
Acipenseridae

The Great Sturgeon, the first representative of the sturgeon family, is the biggest European freshwater fish. It usually grows to a length of 1—3 m, but the largest specimen known measured 5 m and weighed about 1,524 kg. It has 11—15 bony plates (scutes) down its ash-grey back, 40—60 along its lighter sides and 9—12 on its whitish belly. It has a short, wide head and a large, semicircular ventral mouth preceded by flat, fleshy barbels with fine, dense appendages on them.

It is an anadromous fish of the Black Sea, the Sea of Azov and the Caspian Sea; it also occurs in the Adriatic. When migrating it enters the Volga, Ural, Terek, Kura, Danube, Dnestr, Don, Dnepr, Bug and other rivers flowing into the Black and Caspian Seas and the Sea of Azov; it also enters the river Po, which empties into the Adriatic. At one time it travelled up the Danube as far as Passau, but today its main spawning grounds are in the lower and middle reaches of that river.

The Great Sturgeon is an extremely prolific fish and the number of eggs ranges from 300,000 to 7,500,000, according to the size of the female. Males attain sexual maturity at the age of 12—14 years, females not until they are

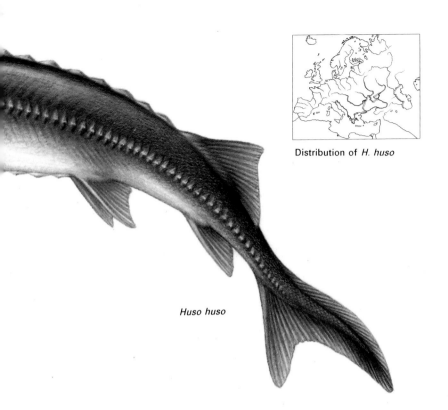

Huso huso

16—18 years old. Sexually mature Great Sturgeons spawn only once in 2—4 years, in the spring or the autumn. Fish which migrate upstream in the autumn 'hibernate', as it were, on a clayey or muddy bed in deep water. The female attaches the eggs to stones on the bottom. The embryos hatch in 8—9 days at a water temperature of 12—14 °C and soon make their way downstream to the sea. At first they live on small freshwater and marine invertebrates; when bigger they subsist almost entirely on fish. Their main prey in the Black Sea is the Anchovy (*Engraulis encrasicholus*); in the Caspian sea they live on marine gobies, herring and various cyprinid fishes.

In addition to the typical form occurring in the Danube, three more subspecies have been described — *H. h. orientalis* in the eastern part of the Black Sea and the relevant rivers, *H. h. maeoticus* in the Sea of Azov and *H. h. caspicus* in the Caspian Sea. The views of ichthyologists on whether this differentiation is warranted are at variance.

The Great Sturgeon is an economically important fish. Its most valued product is its roe, the famous Beluga caviar; its flesh is less in demand.

During the past few decades the Great Sturgeon has been a centre of interest and negotiation among those concerned with its protection in the countries where it occurs. By crossing female Great Sturgeons with male Sterlets they have obtained hybrids which grow much faster and to a bigger size than Sterlets; these hybrids are suitable for breeding in ponds and are also transplanted to open water.

Distribution of *A. sturio*

Acipenser güldenstädti

Common Sturgeon
Acipenser sturio L.

● ○
Sturgeon
Acipenseridae

The Common Sturgeon is a big fish with a bluish grey to greyish green back surmounted by a row of 10—13 light scutes with a raised centre, which in young fish often tapers off to a spine; there are 24—40 scutes on its silvery sides and 11—13 on its white belly. On the under side of its long, pointed head it has a protrusible, almost square mouth which takes up roughly two thirds of the width of its snout. Its barbels are round

in cross section and have no appendages. The first ray of its pectoral fins is strikingly thick. The Common Sturgeon usually measures 1.5—2.5 m, but can grow to a length of over 3 m and weigh over 200 kg.

This anadromous migratory fish is to be found from North Cape, across the sea, down the Atlantic coast of Europe and from the Mediterranean to the Black Sea and the Sea of Azov; it also

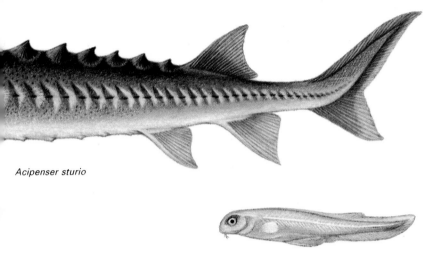

Acipenser sturio

A larva of *A. sturio*

occurs in the Baltic and in Lakes Onega and Ladoga (the latter is probably inhabited by a resident freshwater form).

It migrates up European rivers from April to May and from June to July it spawns in deep pits which it excavates in gravel right in the course of a fast river. In this the female deposits 400,000 to 2,500,000 eggs. The fry, which hatch in 3—5 days and measure about 10 mm, remain in fresh water for 1—3 years. Here, and during the first part of their life in the sea, they live on benthic invertebrates; adult Sturgeons also catch small fish. The Common Sturgeon remains in the sea for a minimum of 7—8 years, males reaching sexual maturity at 7—9 years and females at 8—14 years. They then migrate up the rivers to spawn returning to the sea afterwards.

Once an abundant fish in the rivers of western and central Europe, the only place where the Common Sturgeon is of any economic significance today is the Black Sea. Its blackish gray caviar is particularly in demand. In most big European rivers the Common Sturgeon population has been decimated partly by intensive fishing and partly by high dams and steadily increasing pollution.

The Russian Sturgeon (*Acipenser güldenstädti*), an inhabitant of the Black and Caspian seas and the Sea of Azov, is another big European sturgeon. At spawning time it migrates up the rivers flowing into these seas; in the Danube it actually swims as far as Bratislava in Slovakia, although its numbers there are rapidly dwindling. Unlike the Common Sturgeon, it has a relatively short, blunt snout and a small, straight mouth. Its back is blackish grey to greyish green and its sides and belly are dingy white. It usually measures 130—150 cm and weighs 20—30 kg, but specimens up to 4 m long and weighing over 150 kg are occasionally caught.

It is an anadromous migratory fish and in June it spawns in deep water on sand or gravel, or on sandbanks in estuaries. It probably also occurs in some rivers as a resident freshwater fish. Its diet consists of invertebrate animals and fish. In the Caspian and Black Sea region it is of economic importance.

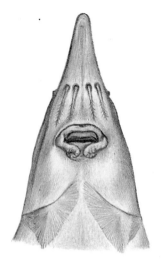

Distribution of *A. ruthenus*

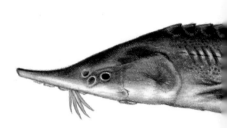

View of the underside of the head of
A. ruthenus

Sterlet
Acipenser ruthenus L.

●○
Sturgeon
Acipenseridae

This small sturgeon, which is about 1 m long and weighs about 10 kg, occurs almost entirely in fresh water and has a long, narrow and pointed snout. On its greyish green or brownish green back it has a row of 11—17 scutes, each tapering upwards to a long, sharp spike. Down its lighter sides there is a row of 60—70 overlapping rhomboid plates and on its pale yellow or pinkish white belly a row of 10—18 plates. Round its mouth it has several conspicuous warty tubercles, with the relatively long, tufted barbels in front of them. The Sterlet's fins—especially the pectoral fins—are relatively long and thick.

The Sterlet is a freshwater migratory fish and the only place where it penetrates into brackish water is the northern part of the Caspian Sea. It occurs in the rivers flowing into the Black and Caspian seas and the Sea of Azov and in some flowing into the Baltic (the Dvina).

In the spring, in the breeding season, it often undertakes long migrations upstream; for instance, before the Linz dam was built on the Danube, it migrated beyond Ulm. It spawns on a gravelly or coarsely sandy bed. The fry are hatched in 4—5 days and remain a relatively long time in shallow water, where they live mainly on the larvae of different aquatic insects (mayflies, stoneflies, gnats, caddis-flies, etc) and later on small fish as well. They spend the winter in depressions in the bed of the river.

Economically, the Sterlet is a very important fish and its flesh is highly prized. Hybrids resulting from crossings of the Sterlet with other sturgeons grow

46

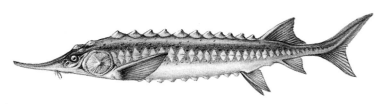

Acipenser stellatus

Acipenser ruthenus

relatively quickly. In some places the Sterlet is also kept as a secondary fish in ponds.

The Starry Sturgeon (*Acipenser stellatus* Pallas) is a further small species; its slightly curved snout is even longer and thinner than the Sterlet's, from which it also differs in respect of its much smaller number of lateral scutes (30—40), which do not overlap one another. Its slender body is circular in cross section. Its back and sides are dark grey to black and its belly is greyish yellow. It grows to an average length of about 1 m (in exceptional cases up to 190 cm) and weighs up to 10 kg or over.

The Starry Sturgeon is an anadromous marine species which migrates from the Black and Caspian seas and the Sea of Aral; very rarely it also appears in the Adriatic and the Aegean Sea, from which it penetrates into the river Maritza. At spawning time it mostly favours the lower reaches of the rivers, but isolated specimens sometimes swim far upstream against the current (in the Danube, for example, as far as Bratislava). As in the case of the Great Sturgeon, spawning migration takes place in the spring or the autumn. The spawning sites generally lie in estuaries, but quite often in shallow parts of the sea. Starry Sturgeons spawn from June to September and stick the eggs to stones in gravel-beds; the fry are hatched in 2—4 days. Soon after hatching the young fish let the current carry them down to the sea. They first of all live on small invertebrates but later on add small fish to the menu.

Distribution of
A. nudiventris (blue)
and *A. naccari* (red)

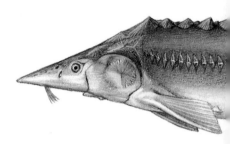

Ship Sturgeon
Acipenser nudiventris LOVETZKY

●◖
Sturgeon
Acipenseridae

As distinct from other members of the family, this sturgeon has a conspicuously thick, short, robust body and an undivided continuous lower lip. Its dark brown to ash grey back is surmounted by a row of 12—15 dorsal scutes with recurved tips. The sides are lighter and its belly is almost white. It has a short snout; the barbels in front of its ventral mouth are round in cross section and have fine appendages on their inner surface. The relatively long dorsal fin is situated right at the end of the body, just in front of the caudal fin. *A. nudiventris* grows to an average length of 1—1.5 m and weighs about 10 kg; the biggest specimens known measured 2 m and weighed 40—50 kg.

A. nudiventris is a migratory anadromous fish inhabiting the Black Sea, the Sea of Azov, the southern part of the Caspian Sea and the Sea of Aral. Danubian fish form a freshwater population and never migrate seawards; in the spawning season, however, they under-

take long journeys up the Danube and its large tributaries. Spawning takes place early in the spring, from February to May, on a gravelly bed in the higher, fast and deep reaches of the rivers. The economic importance of this fish for production is greatest in the region of the Sea of Aral and its tributary rivers, where it has also been studied in the greatest detail. It was found that the fish entered the rivers in the autumn, spent the winter in their deepest parts and then spawned in flowing water. *A. nudiventris* lives mainly on invertebrate animals (in particular aquatic molluscs) and occasionally on fish, but the Aral form takes no food during its sojourn in the rivers. Since in the Caspian and Black seas it is not considered to be of any great importance, the biology of this sturgeon in those waters has received less attention.

Relatively little is known about the last species, the Adriatic Sturgeon, *Acipenser naccari* Bonaparte, which has

Acipenser nudiventris

Acipenser naccari

a basically olive grey back and a light grey belly. Down its back runs a row of 12—14 scutes and down its sides 40—42 scutes. Unlike the snout of other sturgeons, the upper part of its rounded and relatively long snout is ossified. Its very long, smooth barbels are situated well forwards on the under side of its head, close to the snout, and are quite a long way away from the inferior mouth. The Adriatic Sturgeon can measure 1—2 m and exceptionally weigh about 40 kg, but its usual length and weight are 1—1.5 m and 10—15 kg respectively.

In the breeding season, this scarce and comparatively unknown sturgeon spawns in the river Po and in several other rivers emptying into the northern part of the Adriatic.

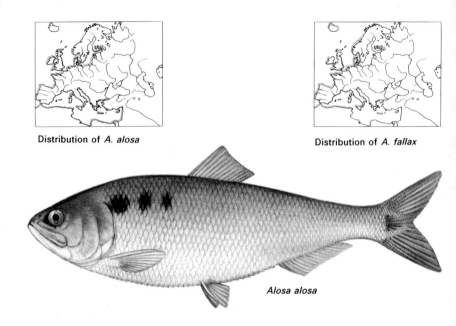

Distribution of *A. alosa*

Distribution of *A. fallax*

Alosa alosa

Allis Shad
Alosa alosa (L.)

●◐○
Herrings
Clupeidae

Herrings are mostly sea-fish but the Allis Shad is a migratory anadromous species.

It is 50—70 cm long and has a bluish green back, a golden-brown head and silvery, gleaming-gold sides and belly. On the upper edge of each operculum there is a black spot and behind this, in line with it, one or two more spots on each side of the body. Down the belly runs a sharp, scaly ridge. The Allis Shad lives in the North Sea, from the south-west coast of Norway as far as the western part of the Mediterranean; it does not occur in the Baltic.

In the spring it migrates up European rivers and spawns in May and June in clean, well-oxygenated water in their upper reaches. The eggs float above the bed and the embryos are hatched in 4—5 days. When the fry measure about 10 cm, they are carried downstream to

the sea. They spend several years in the sea, but when they measure 30—40 cm and reach adulthood, they migrate in the spring to fresh water to spawn for the first time. In the sea the Allis Shad lives on various planktonic crustaceans; while migrating it goes without food.

At the beginning of the twentieth century, this fish, together with Salmon and Sea Trout, was still to be seen deep inland in the Rhine and the Elbe—in the Rhine as far as Basle and in the Elbe and Vltava beyond Prague. Since then, numerous construction works and a high degree of pollution have finally put an end to the Allis Shad's visits to these rivers.

Two subspecies of this fish have been described—*Alosa alosa macedonica* in the Aegean Sea and *A. alosa bulgarica* in the Black Sea.

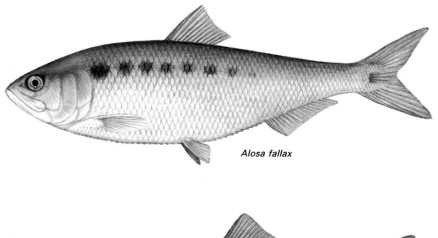

Alosa fallax

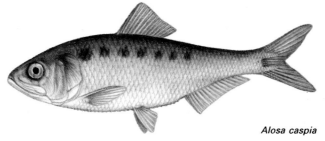

Alosa caspia

Twaite Shad; Finta Shad
Alosa fallax (Lacépède)

● ◑ ○
Herrings
Clupeidae

The Twaite Shad is smaller than the Allis Shad, but has more dark spots along its sides (usually 4—8). Unlike the Allis Shad, it occurs down the whole length of the coast of Europe, together with a large part of the Baltic and the Mediterranean, but at spawning time it goes no further than the lower reaches of the rivers. It spawns in June and July. Several subspecies have been described in various parts of Europe, including freshwater forms in Alpine lakes (Lago Maggiore, Lago di Garda, etc).

In the Black Sea, the Sea of Azov and the Caspian Sea we can encounter the related Caspian Shad, *Alosa* (*Caspialosa*) *caspia* (Eichwald), which is only about 30 cm long. It is an economically important fish in this region, especially in the northern parts of the Caspian Sea. These fish spawn mostly in the spring, in relatively cold water at a depth of 2—4 m, in the uppermost reaches of rivers flowing into the Caspian Sea and the Black Sea. Several subspecies are known. Closely related to the shads is the Tyulka Sardelle, *Clupeonella delicatula* (Nordmann), which is important to the fishing industry in the above seas and is also a source of food for larger fishes in the region.

Large shads are often predatory; smaller species live on pelagic plankton.

View of the head of a male *S. salar*

Distribution of *S. salar*

View of the head of a female *S. salar*

A young fish (fry)

Atlantic Salmon
Salmo salar L.

●◑○■
Salmonids
Salmonidae

The large Atlantic Salmon, which in exceptional cases measures as much as 1.5 m and weighs over 30 kg, can be distinguished from the similar and related Sea Trout by its relatively small head, its slightly concave caudal fin and its reddish grey (in the Sea Trout red-edged) adipose fin. Its operculum and suboperculum are not in contact with the preoperculum.

The Atlantic Salmon is an anadromous migratory fish. While migrating, the males become darker, reddish spots appear on their sides, their belly turns pink and their lower jaw is hooked; the females remain silvery grey. The Atlantic Salmon lives in the Atlantic Ocean, including the North Sea and the Baltic.

The young Salmon, known as 'alevins', hatch in April or May in the cold, well-oxygenated parts of mountain rivers, and are about 2 cm long. For about the first 40 days they subsist on the contents of their large yolk sac; when that is absorbed, they are known as 'fry' and live on planktonic crustaceans, insect larvae and (later) small fish. The young Salmon remain 2—5 years in fresh water during which time they are known as 'parr'. Eventually their back turns greyish green and their sides and belly silvery white and as 'smolt' they set out on their long journey down to the sea. The Salmon inhabiting certain Swedish lakes and lakes Ladoga and Onega are an exception, since they are resident

52

A young specimen of *Salmo salar* ('smolt')

Salmo salar ♂

freshwater forms and include dwarf males which already attain sexual maturity at a length of only 10 cm.

Salmon remain 1—4 years in the sea, where they live on fish (herrings, etc) and grow much faster than in fresh water. Their flesh contains a large amount of fat and turns 'salmon' pink. When fully grown and nicely fattened, they migrate back up the rivers in which they were spawned, guided by the chemistry of the water. On the way they overcome the most diverse obstacles, some of them over 4 m long and 1.5 m high, such as weirs, waterfalls and raging rapids. In the upper reaches, in cold, strongly flowing water rich in oxygen, the females excavate redds in a sandy and gravelly bed, in which they deposit up to 30,000 eggs 4—7 mm in diameter.

With movements of their body and caudal fin, the fish bury the fertilized eggs in the gravel and sand to keep them safe from enemies. Most of the adult salmon die of exhaustion when they have finished spawning and only a small minority return to the sea and are able to spawn a second time.

The Salmon is commercially important, but because of pollution and the building of various constructions, its numbers in European rivers are steadily diminishing and in the German rivers flowing into the North Sea (the Elbe, Weser and Rhine) it has practically disappeared altogether. Greater numbers can still be caught in Scotland, Ireland and Scandinavia. Salmon are a very highly prized fish with anglers, who catch it by trolling or fly-fishing.

Distribution of
S. t. trutta

Salmo trutta trutta

Sea Trout
Salmo trutta trutta L.

●◑○
Salmonids
Salmonidae

The Sea Trout is a handsome salmonid fish whose biology is similar to that of the Atlantic Salmon. Its back is greyish (the female) or brownish (the male) and it has lighter sides and a silvery belly. On its head, sides and back there are numerous black spots which in breeding colour often have a yellow border and are linked by red spots. The Sea Trout has a more robust body and a relatively larger head than the Atlantic Salmon. Its caudal fin is straight-edged and not concave and its adipose fin has a red border, while in the Atlantic Salmon it is a uniform greyish red. Like young Salmon, young Sea Trout have dark cross stripes and have red spots on their body. The operculum and suboperculum are in contact with the preoperculum. The Sea Trout grows to a length of over 1 m and a weight in excess of 30 kg.

The Sea Trout occurs in the coastal waters of the Atlantic, the North Sea and the Baltic; in Europe it is to be found from the mouth of the river Duoro in Portugal to the Arctic Ocean. It is an anadromous fish and spawns from December to March in redds which are similar to those of the Atlantic Salmon, but lie further upstream. It generally leaves the sea for the rivers in June or July, but sometimes not until the autumn. Its migration tends to be less extensive and less exhausting than the Salmon's, so it is able to spawn several times in the course of its life.

The eggs are covered with gravel, like those of the Salmon. When the young fish measure 10—20 cm they lose their cross stripes and spots, their sides turn silvery and they migrate seawards.

Experiments have shown that if the Sea Trout is unable to escape from

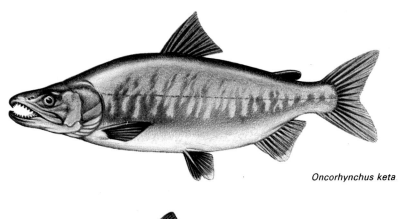

Oncorhynchus keta

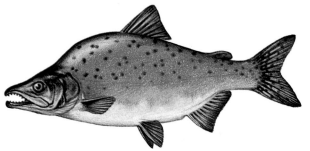

Oncorhynchus gorbuscha

fresh water to the sea, it becomes a Brown Trout or a Lake Trout; conversely, young Brown and Lake Trout, in the sea, become typical Sea Trout and at spawning time migrate to fresh water. The three are thus not separate species, but are at most subspecies. Many authorities do not even consider the subspecies should be separated.

The Sea Trout is economically less important than the Atlantic Salmon. In rivers it is caught in the same manner.

The large anadromous fishes of the genus *Oncorhynchus*, which inhabit the northern parts of the Pacific, are also salmonids. In the past, two species — the Humpback Salmon, *O. gorbuscha* (Walbaum) and Chum Salmon, *O. keta* (Walbaum) — have been repeatedly introduced into Arctic and North European seas. During their spawning migration the males of both species have a strikingly hooked lower jaw and a hump on their back. The hump is larger in *O. gorbuscha*, from which it earns its name. These fishes usually grow to a length of about 70 cm; at the age of 2—4 years migrate upstream to spawn and die after spawning. They are of considerable economic significance in the Pacific waters of the USSR, Japan, the USA and Canada.

S. t. fario juv.

Brown Trout
Salmo trutta fario L.

○ ■
Salmonids
Salmonidae

This typical salmonid fish of European mountain streams, rivers and lakes is very brightly and variably coloured. Immature specimens have large, distinct bluish grey spots on their sides; the adult trout have red spots (often with a light border) on their dark back and lighter sides. The light-coloured adipose fin has dark edges and is usually red at the tip. The trout's belly is yellowish white to yellow.

The Brown Trout lives in well-oxygenated mountain and submontane streams and rivers throughout the whole of Europe. Fish living in rivers emptying into the North Sea and the Baltic belong to the subspecies *S. t. fario* and those in rivers flowing into the Black Sea to the subspecies *S. t. labrax*. The differences between the two subspecies are negligible, however, and have been largely obliterated by distribution and artificial introduction into various suitable types of water all over Europe. The rivers emptying into the Mediterranean are inhabited by the subspecies *S. t. macrostigma*. Some authorities do not consider that any subspecies can be reliably recognized.

In adulthood, male trout often have a strikingly curved lower jaw, while the females have a shorter head than the males. A spawning female is generally accompanied by several males; when the eggs have been fertilized it covers them with sand and gravel. The newly hatched fry have a large yolk sac as a source of food for the first days of life. When this has been consumed they catch small insect larvae and crustaceans; bigger trout prefer insects which have fallen on to the water and small fish.

The Brown Trout is an economically very important freshwater fish. It is a popular fish with anglers, to whom

Salmo trutta fario ♀

Salmo trutta fario ♂

catching it with a fly is an experience of the highest order. Brown trout have been bred in cold ponds and artificial hatcheries for several centuries; today, in many European countries, the latter method is the only way of ensuring that this valuable fish will still remain in their mountain streams. Brown trout have also been introduced successfully into dam reservoirs; here, however, they soon changed to the large lake form, which spawns in the tributary streams. The Brown Trout is likewise bred in some carp ponds with an adequate flow of water and here it is caught with nets. It grows to a length of 50 cm and weighs up to 2 kg and sometimes more.

Many systems are used for breeding the Brown Trout artificially. It spawns in the winter (from January to March) and the newly hatched fry (fingerlings) are reared in special circular growing ponds. For the past few decades a special diet has been used to speed up their growth. The Brown Trout can be set free in open water at the age of one or two years.

View of the head of a female *S. t. lacustris*

Lake Trout
Salmo trutta lacustris L.

○ ■
Salmonids
Salmonidae

The Lake Trout is a form which is especially plentiful in mountain lakes or dam reservoirs. Nowadays, we can observe how small Brown Trout introduced into upland lakes develop into this large lake form. Their transformation is accompanied by a colour change; the bright colouring of the Brown Trout alters to a uniform silver and the characteristic red spots disappear, leaving the head, back and sides marked only with black spots. In some lakes the Lake Trout actually grow to a larger size than the Sea Trout, which it closely resembles. The Lake Trout is not considered as a subspecies distinct from Brown or Sea Trout by many authorities.

In Europe, Lake Trout are distributed chiefly in Alpine lakes at altitudes of up to more than 2,000 m; they also live in Lake Constance (the Bodensee) in Switzerland and in many lakes in northern England, northern Scotland, Wales and Ireland. Since dams have been built on the upper reaches of rivers, Lake Trout also frequently appear today in the resultant large reservoirs; the Orava dam in northern Slovakia and the Lipno dam in southern Bohemia can be taken as

examples. Particularly large Lake Trout are to be found in Alpine lakes situated at high altitudes.

The Lake Trout is partly a migratory fish which spawns in streams which feed and drain large lakes. Trout living in Lake Geneva migrate first of all along the Rhône and then up the river Arve (a tributary of the Rhône) to their spawning grounds. In many Alpine lakes the trout spawn directly on the bottom, often at considerable depths, where underground springs ensure that the sand is kept continuously washed. Lake Trout spawn from September to December and the only exceptions are those in Lake Garda in northern Italy, which spawn in the summer. The latter are regarded by some as a separate subspecies and sometimes even as a separate species (*S. t. carpione* or *S. carpio*).

Young Lake Trout remain 1—3 years in the place where they hatched and then make their way to the lake, where at first they live in the upper layers of the water and are considered to be immature, non-fertile forms; later on they retire to deep water.

Growth of the Lake Trout varies con-

Salmo trutta lacustris ♂

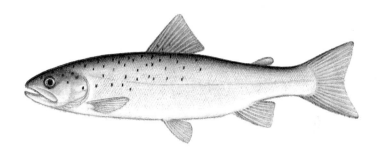

A silvery sterile form of *S. t. lacustris*

siderably with locality. In some lakes its weight does not exceed 5 kg, while in others it can measure 1.5 m and weigh over 30 kg. Similarly, in some waters it becomes sexually mature in its third year and yet in others not until its seventh.

The Lake Trout is an economically important fish in the Alpine countries and in Great Britain. During their migration the fish are caught with nets, but while they are in the lake they are caught by anglers with artificial flies or spoon lures. In most lakes, however, and especially in the Alps, the existence of this handsome and noble fish is endangered by the various constructions built on the streams in which they spawn and by increasing pollution from newly built-up areas in the vicinity.

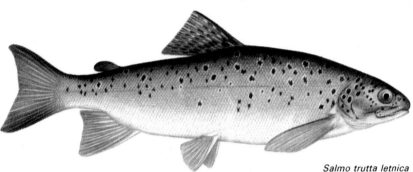

Salmo trutta letnica

○ ■
Salmonids
Salmonidae

Salmo trutta letnica (KARAMAN)

In the Macedonian part of south-western Yugoslavia, bordering on Albania and separated by the Galichitsa massif, lie two mountain lakes, Prespa and Ohrid. The latter (altitude 698 m) is particularly famous as an international nature reserve, whose unique fauna and flora developed independently of the plants and animals of the surrounding regions from the Tertiary Era onwards. The lake is 30 km long, 15 km wide and up to 286 m deep. Since it lies in an extensive karst range and is fed largely by underground springs, its water is incredibly clean and is transparent to a depth of about 20 m. Its water—both shallow and deep—is inhabited by a distinctive endemic fish fauna.

The most famous of the fishes in Lake Ohrid is undoubtedly the large lake trout *S. t. letnica*, which measures up to 1.5 m, can weigh over 20 kg and forms several races differing from one another in respect of when and where they spawn. Its economic significance is enormous, since it accounts for 43% of all the fish caught in the lake. Lake Ohrid fishermen catch it in large, deep seines and also in nylon gill-nets with meshes measuring 4.5 × 4.5 cm, let down to a depth of 80 m. Angling is permitted once a month from motorboats, with spinners.

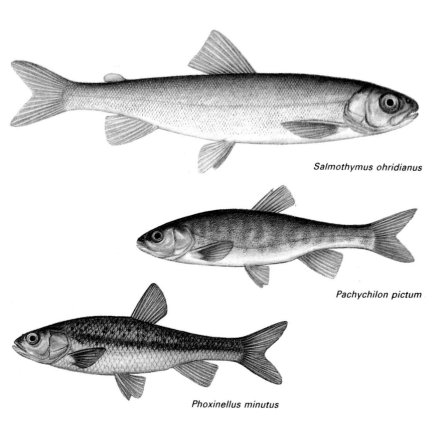

Salmothymus ohridianus

Pachychilon pictum

Phoxinellus minutus

Adriatic Salmon
Salmothymus (Acantoligna) ohridianus
(STEINDACHNER)

Salmothymus ohridianus is a deep-water salmonid fish inhabiting Lake Ohrid. It has a relatively slim, flat-sided body, a small head, tiny teeth, a noticeably blunt snout and silvery sides; it grows to a length of 50 cm and weighs about 1 kg. Lake Ohrid fishermen catch it in fine nylon gill nets 40 m long, 1 m high and with meshes 2.5×2.5 cm, which they usually lower to a depth of about 40 m.

In addition to these two economically valuable salmonids, Lake Ohrid contains many other endemic fishes, such as *Pachychilon pictum* (Heckel et Kner) and

Phoxinellus minutus (Karaman) (two cyprinid species) and a whole series of endemic subspecies of other fish (e.g. Roach, Chub, Minnow, Rudd, Nase, Gudgeon, Barbel, Bleak and Stone Loach). Lake Ohrid is also well stocked with carp and masses of bleak are caught by hook and nets. Eels are caught in a special permanent trap situated on the lake's sole effluent river— the Black Drin. On an average, 220 tons of fish are caught in this unique Balkan lake every year.

View of the head of a female *S. gairdneri*

Distribution of *S. gairdneri*

Rainbow Trout
Salmo gairdneri RICHARDSON

○ ■ □
Salmonids
Salmonidae

Fertilized eggs of the Rainbow Trout, a North American cousin of the European Brown Trout, were first brought to Europe in the 1890's. Originally a migratory anadromous fish of the west coast of North America, in its native region the Rainbow Trout, like the Brown Trout, occurs in several different forms, from a marine migratory anadromous form to a resident freshwater form living permanently in lakes, rivers and streams. Various forms have been imported to Europe. Transplantation of the migratory form to streams and rivers was not a success, because the fish vanished from flowing water. If bred in ponds, however, the migratory form was eventually transformed to a resident form which significantly enriched European waters, since it is far more adaptable than the Brown Trout as regards temperature, food and the oxygen content of the water. Today it is therefore successfully bred in reservoirs, suitable stretches of rivers, ponds and fish farms.

The Rainbow Trout has a bluish grey to greenish grey back and lighter sides with a pink, rainbow-hued stripe running along them. Its back, sides and dorsal, caudal and adipose fin are dotted with large numbers of small dark spots. This species grows to an average length of about 35 cm and weighs roughly 1 kg, but in exceptional cases can measure 70 cm and weigh up to 7 kg. Its food at first consists of small invertebrates (plankton) and later of various benthic animals, small fish and insects floating on the surface. Big specimens are particularly fond of fish, but willingly also accept substitute food (granules, etc).

Where the water is rich in food the Rainbow Trout grows very quickly and within three years can weigh up to 1 kg. It attains sexual maturity in its second or third year. In the breeding season (from December to May), like other salmonids it excavates redds in sand and gravel in the upper reaches of rivers and streams. In these, with the aid of its

S. gairdneri juv.

Salmo gairdneri ♂

body and fins, it buries its 500—5,000 relatively large eggs, which take 100—150 days to develop, according to the temperature of the water.

The Rainbow Trout is an economically important fish. Being a 'single portion' trout it is a popular delicacy and is therefore bred artificially in most European countries; pond-bred specimens already weigh the necessary 200—250 g by their second year. At the age of one or two years rainbow trout are often transferred to open water (rivers, streams, reservoirs and sometimes suitable lakes), where they are available to anglers. They are caught with spinners, a dead fish or sometimes with a fly. The transfer of Rainbow Trout to open water is not always successful, however, since migratory populations escape from streams and rivers.

Distribution of
S. alpinus

View of the head of a female *S. alpinus*

Charr
Salvelinus alpinus (L.)

Young Charrs have a slim body and, like other young salmonids, they have 13—15 dark cross stripes on their sides. Older, sexually mature specimens are very distinctively coloured, especially at spawning time; they have a light blue back, greyish blue or greenish sides marked with small, round red or orange spots, a bright red belly and a yellow throat; the first rays of their pectoral, ventral and anal fins are gleaming white. Out of the spawning season their colours are less striking and their belly is silvery. They have very small scales.

The Charr is an anadromous marine fish which migrates inland in the autumn to spawn; it occurs in the Arctic region of Europe, Asia and North America. The young fish remain in fresh water for three or four years and leave it in the winter, when they generally migrate seawards under the ice. Very often they do not reach their destination until June. In fresh water the Charr lives mainly on invertebrate animals (insect

larvae, worms and insects floating on the surface of the water or flying just above it), but its chief food in the sea are fish, especially cod. At the age of six or seven years the Charr leaves the sea for the rivers to spawn for the first time. By then it usually measures 50—60 cm and weighs 1.5—2 kg, although in exceptional cases we may come across specimens weighing up to 15 kg.

The lakes of Sweden, Finland and Norway, many lakes in the Alps, England, Ireland and Scotland, on Iceland and Spitsbergen (Svalbard), lakes Ladoga and Onega and others are inhabited by a multitude of resident freshwater forms of the Charr; in Europe alone there are over twenty. At one time they were described as separate species or subspecies, but today they are considered to be special races closely related to the migratory Arctic Charr. Some of them spawn in the littoral zone of the lake, others in deep water. The race *S. a. salvelinus* lives in Alpine lakes in the

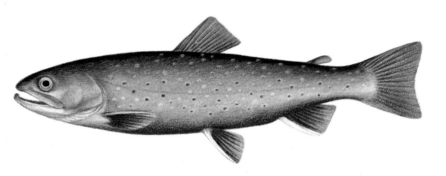

A male *Salvelinus alpinus* at spawning time

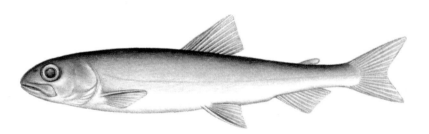

A deep-water form of *Salvelinus alpinus*

Danube basin, *S. a. umbla* in Alpine lakes in the basins of the Rhine and the Rhône, *S. a. salmarinus* in Italian Alpine lakes and *S. a. lepeschini* in lakes Onega and Ladoga. Lake Constance and some of the higher lakes in the Alps are inhabited by a small deep-water form of the Charr, which is soberly coloured and has conspicuously large eyes.

The Charr is an economically important fish, especially in Arctic regions. It is caught while migrating, with wicker traps and other types of nets. In lakes it is prized by anglers, who catch it by spinning or with flies.

Distribution of
S. fontinalis

Brook Charr
Salvelinus fontinalis (Mitchill)

■ □
Salmonids
Salmonidae

The Brook Charr originally came from the eastern part of the USA (Maine) and Canada (Labrador) and was introduced into Europe at the end of the 19th century. It is usually 20—35 (occasionally up to 50) cm long and weighs up to 3 kg. Its mouth, which is larger than that of the Charr, always stretches beyond its eyes (in the Charr it finishes just below the eyes). This fish has a powerful, stream-lined, slightly flat-sided body with a greenish brown, light-mottled back, greenish yellow sides covered with yellow, green and red spots and an orange-red belly. Its caudal and dorsal fins are light olive and the former is marked with black spots. The pectoral, ventral and anal fins are orange and their first rays are white, with a black border.

The Brook Charr is a resident freshwater fish inhabiting cold, swiftly flowing streams and rivers. Its habits are similar to those of the Brown Trout and the Charr, with which it can interbreed. The Brook Charr spawns from October to March and makes a dish-like redd in sand in a strong current in the upper reaches of rivers. Since it lives on a diet of benthic invertebrate animals, insects and occasional small fish, it competes for food with the Brown Trout and the Charr.

In central Europe the Brook Charr grows relatively quickly and to a good size. In Štrbské Pleso in the Tatra Mountains in Slovakia we can find specimens measuring 50 cm and weighing up to 3 kg. Populations in some of the higher streams in the Giant Mountains in northern Bohemia have survived for many years. In the river Elbe it lives in a relatively short stretch of the river, from the waterfall to the place where the Elbe tumbles over the rocks to the lower part of the valley. In the acid peaty water, where the Brown Trout would never survive, the Brook Charr spawns every year and a healthy population persists. The Brook Charr was also introduced into many lakes in the Alps; in some of them it disappeared after a time, while in others it became established.

At present, the economic importance of the Brook Charr in Europe is small, but it is a suitable fish for the colonisation of acid and other waters at high altitudes unsuitable for the Brown Trout. Occasionally it is bred in trout hatcheries and set free in flowing water and convenient lakes, where it is very popular with anglers. It is caught with a spoon lure, by spin-and-draw method with a dead fish or a fly.

The front of the body of a female
S. fontinalis

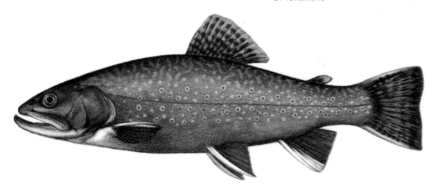

Salvelinus fontinalis ♂

A hybrid of *Salvelinus fontinalis*
× *Salmo trutta fario*

Distribution of
H. hucho (blue) and
H. taimen (red)

Hucho hucho juv.

Danube Salmon; Huchen
Hucho hucho (L.)

■
Salmonids
Samonidae

The Danube Salmon is a permanent inhabitant of the mountain and submontane parts of the Danube and its tributaries. It grows to a length of over 120 cm and weighs up to 50 kg. It has a long, slightly flat-topped head and the corners of its mouth lie well behind its eyes. Its back is brownish red or brownish green to greyish brown (often with a violet sheen), its sides are pinkish and its belly is white. Its sides and back are sprinkled with large numbers of small blackish grey spots. Young Danube salmon are silvery and resemble young trout. Except for the adipose fin, the fins are relatively small and there are often a few dark spots on the dorsal and caudal fin.

The Danube Salmon is a resident of large, swift rivers of the Danubian system at high and submontane altitudes and is occasionally to be found in lakes near the mouth of rivers. It spawns at temperatures of 6—9 °C, usually from March to May and generally as soon as the winter snows have melted, travelling long distances upstream to do so. It excavates a large, deep redd in sand and afterwards covers the fertilized eggs. In the spawning season the males develop a hooked lower jaw.

Initially, young Danube Salmon feed on aquatic insect larvae and other invertebrate animals, but after they reach 5—6 cm they begin to catch fish. The adults feed almost exclusively on fish and display a special predilection for the silvery Danubian Nase. The Danube Salmon is a typical territorial fish and tolerates no competitors within the bounds of its domain; it generally hides away in deep mountain pools under exposed roots, in the shade of a rock or large boulder and often in a raging current. It attacks like lightning, with a great deal of noise, and frequently pursues its prey right to the bank.

Hucho hucho

Hucho taimen

Being extremely sensitive to pollution and oxygen deficiency, in recent years it has begun to disappear rapidly from many places where it was once relatively abundant. In some European countries it is bred and reared artificially in cold ponds with a constant flow of water, where the fish receive supplementary food; they are then used to stock suitable rivers.

Although of little economic significance, the Danube Salmon is very popular with anglers and to land one gives the angler an immense thrill. Danube Salmon are caught by spinning, using dead bait or a spoon lure, and with flies. Playing one in the winter, with the great fish fighting tenaciously for its life, is undoubtedly a supreme experience for an angler.

The related Siberian species the Taimen, *Hucho taimen* (Pallas), which measures 150 cm and weighs up to 60 kg (in exceptional cases as much as 80 kg) extends into Europe from the east and is to be found in the Volga and the Ural, as well as in the great Siberian rivers and their tributaries.

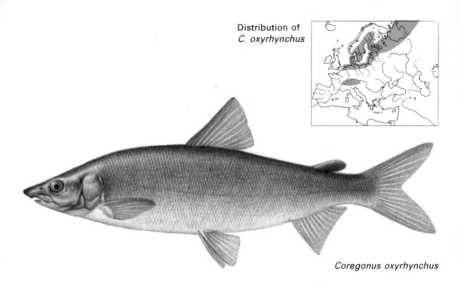

Distribution of
C. oxyrhynchus

Coregonus oxyrhynchus

Houting
Coregonus oxyrhynchus (L.)

● ○
Whitefishes
Coregonidae

Like the Freshwater Houting, the Houting belongs to a group of five large whitefishes living in European waters. It has 36—44 gill-rakers on its first branchial arch, a long, slightly flat-sided body and a pointed snout with an inferior mouth. Its back is greyish blue to bluish green and its sides and belly are pearly white. It is likewise a very plastic fish and in addition to large and quickly growing forms there are dwarf forms which are often mistaken for Vendace. The Houting is mostly a resident lake fish, although a migratory form occurs in the Elbe and the Rhine; it is distributed in the same area as the Freshwater Houting. It grows to a length of 50 cm. Its economic importance is steadily declining, but small quantities are still caught with nets in the lower Elbe and Rhine. It is likewise to be found in Lake Constance, the basin of the river Oder, lakes Ladoga and Onega, England, Ireland and many other places, where it

has hitherto been known everywhere under other specific names.

Of the other three, very variable whitefishes in this group, the Arctic Whitefish, *Coregonus pidschian* (Gmelin), inhabits the Arctic region and cold Alpine lakes at high altitudes. It generally spawns from September to January in rivers or near the edge of the lake and seldom at any great depth. It is often accompanied by the similar Broad Whitefish, *C. nasus* (Pallas), which likewise occurs in Alpine lakes, in the lakes of northern Germany, Poland and Scandinavia and in lakes Ladoga and Onega and is further known as an anadromous fish in the Baltic.

The Siberian Cisco or Northern Whitefish, *C. peled* (Gmelin), one of the very largest whitefishes, is characterized by a large number of gill-rakers (45—68). It is distributed in Finnish and Swedish lakes, in the northern part of the USSR and right across the whole of

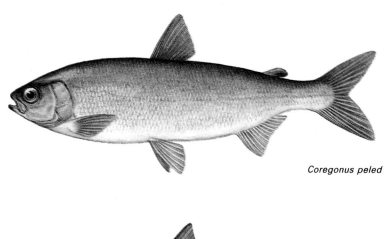

Coregonus peled

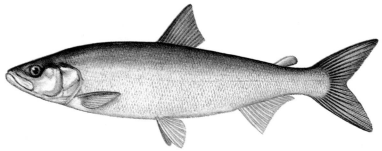

Stenodus leucichthys

Siberia as far as the river Kolyma. In the east it can weigh up to 14 kg, but it usually measures 60—70 cm and weighs 1—2 kg. In this species we also find normal and dwarf populations comprising both freshwater and migratory marine forms.

The only member of the genus *Stenodus*, the Cisco, *S. leucichthys* (Güldenstädt), has a similarly shaped body to the above species. It is an anadromous fish living in the Caspian Sea, grows to a length of over 1 m and weighs up to 20 kg. It has a pointed head, relatively small eyes, a large terminal mouth and

a somewhat protruding lower jaw. The Cisco is a predatory fish, but during its spawning migration, when it travels 3,000 km up the river Volga, it goes without food. Migration takes place in the spring and the autumn. The eggs are deposited on the river bed and as soon as they hatch the fry make their way to the sea, which they usually reach in June. In the Caspian Sea the Cisco mainly frequents very deep water, where it catches gobies, whitefish and various cyprinid fishes. Its economic importance in this region is considerable and it is even bred there artificially.

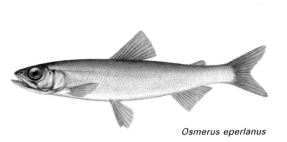

Osmerus eperlanus

Distribution of
C. albula

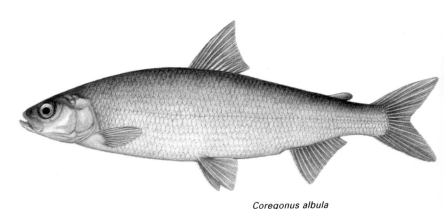

Coregonus albula

Vendace
Coregonus albula L.

● ○
Whitefishes
Coregonidae

The Vendace, a member of the large and systematically complex whitefish family, is a small, slim fish rather like a herring, with an adipose fin, large eyes and a relatively small terminal mouth. It has a bluish green back and its sides and belly are silvery. On its first branchial arch it has 36—52 long, thick gill-rakers. It usually measures about 20 cm and seldom grows to over 35 cm.

This species comprises both resident freshwater lake forms and anadromous forms from the Baltic. The latter migrate upstream to spawn from October to December and stick their eggs to sand and gravel on the river bed. The fry remain near the surface; the larger fish form huge shoals. The Vendace lives entirely on planktonic crustaceans.

The Vendace occurs in northern England and Scotland, Danish and other Scandinavian lakes, lakes Onega and Ladoga, the Volga basin, Polish and German lakes—especially east of the Elbe, e.g. in Mecklenburg—and the Waginersee in Bavaria.

Its economic significance increases in an easterly direction; it is caught during its spawning migration with different types of nets.

The closely related *Coregonus baunti* Muchomedijarov, which lives in Swedish lakes, spawns from April to the end of May in deep water.

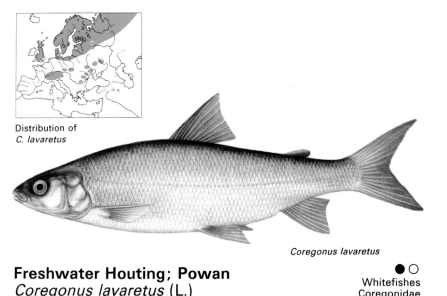

Distribution of
C. lavaretus

Coregonus lavaretus

Freshwater Houting; Powan
Coregonus lavaretus (L.)

● ○
Whitefishes
Coregonidae

The Freshwater Houting is one of the larger whitefishes. In Europe it occurs from Britain in the west, across Scandinavia, northern Germany and northern Poland to the northern parts of the USSR in the east, and it also occurs in many of the lakes in the Alps. It forms a whole series of races which all have one feature in common—their 25—34 gill-rakers. In some places (e.g. in the Baltic), the Freshwater Houting is an anadromous migratory fish; elsewhere (e.g. in Alpine lakes) it is a resident freshwater fish. Here and there we find dwarf populations, whose members measure no more than 10—12 cm, while in other places it grows to a length of up to 50 cm. Migratory forms breed in rivers, freshwater forms above the deepest parts of lakes, usually in the autumn, from October to December.

The Freshwater Houting has very moist, tasty flesh, which is particularly good when smoked.

Smelt
Osmerus eperlanus (L.)

● ○ ▶
Smelts
Osmeridae

Like whitefishes and salmonids, smelts (family Osmeridae) have an adipose fin. The Smelt is a slender, transparent, slightly flat-sided fish not more than 30 cm long, with a very large, gaping mouth and relatively large teeth. In the spawning season, gleaming metallic longitudinal stripes appear on its silvery sides. The Smelt is an anadromous seafish distributed off the Atlantic coast of Europe from the north of Spain to Scandinavia; it also occurs in the Baltic. It is of considerable economic importance, especially as cattle fodder and as raw material for the production of cod liver oil. It is also very often used as bait to catch predatory fish.

Distribution of
T. thymallus

Grayling
Thymallus thymallus (L.)

The Grayling is a gregarious fish of the submontane reaches of rivers with a hard sandy or stony bed. Its range in Europe stretches from western Wales, France and northern Italy (the Po basin) to the White Sea. In Scandinavia it lives in clean lakes, where its existence is now threatened by acid rain. It does not occur in southern Europe, in the north of Scandinavia or in Ireland. In the Alpine rivers it ascends to altitudes of about 1,500 m and in the Carpathians to about 1,000 m.

The Grayling is rather flat-sided and its head is quite small in relation to its body. It also has a relatively small mouth, with tiny teeth, and its upper jaw projects slightly beyond its lower jaw. Its fairly large scales are anchored firmly in the skin. Young Grayling are a silvery light green and have bluish spots on their sides, like young brown trout. Older fish (aged two and three years) have a greyish green back, greenish sides and a white belly. The longitudinal dark stripes on the back (yellowish on the sides) correspond to individual rows of scales. The Grayling's unpaired fins have a mauvish tinge; the long, tall dorsal fin is gaily decorated with a few rows of red and black spots. The whole fish is faintly iridescent. The dorsal, anal and pectoral fins of the male Grayling are larger than those of the female.

Grayling reach sexual maturity in their third or fourth year; they spawn in March and April and sometimes at the beginning of May, when the water temperature rises to 6—8 °C. They spawn in the shallow parts of rivers (at a depth of not more than 50 cm) with a fast current and a coarsely sandy or gravelly bottom. The amber-coloured eggs are smaller than trout eggs. The Grayling buries them in the sand at the spawning site and the tiny fry are hatched in two or three weeks. As distinct from trout and other salmonids, the Grayling's redd is excavated by the male, which defends it against rival males and frequently spawns in it with several females.

The favourite haunts of Grayling are hollows eaten away by the water behind boulders and shady water under overhanging branches or a jutting bank in places where the current skirts a pool. In such spots, several Grayling can often be found together. They live on a variety of invertebrates—mainly aquatic insect larvae, although a substantial part of their diet consists of insects which settle on the water and are caught chiefly in the evening.

In European waters the Grayling grows to a length of over 40 cm and weighs about 1 kg. It has a short life span of only five years (in exceptional cases six).

Its economic significance is relatively

Thymallus thymallus ♂

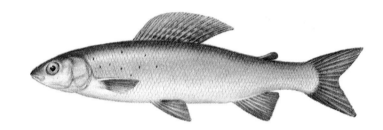

Thymallus thymallus ♀

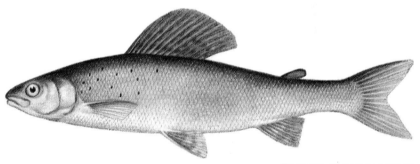

Thymallus arcticus baicalensis

small, but it is one of the most popular fishes with anglers, who generally employ fly lures to catch it.

In recent years a number of attempts have been made to introduce the Baikal species *Thymallus arcticus baicalensis* Dybowski into suitable reservoirs in central Europe and the results to date are quite promising.

Distribution of *E. lucius*

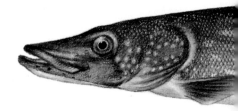

Pike
Esox lucius L.

○ ■
Pike
Esocidae

The Pike's flattened, streamlined body is practically the same width along its entire length. The head is very long and has tapering jaws and a very wide, gaping, flat-topped snout full of teeth. There are no teeth in the upper jaw, but the lower jaw is generously supplied with long, recurved teeth. There are also large numbers of teeth on the palate, the intermaxillary bones, the vomer and the hyoid bone and even the gill arches are thickly covered with minute teeth. The scales are relatively small and oval, and fixed firmly in the skin. The lateral line is well developed and is often inter- rupted. In addition to the main lateral line the Pike has two or three smaller lateral lines along its sides. Together, the tactile pores on the head and jaws and the lateral lines form a perfect 're- mote sensing' organ which replaces vi- sion in turbid water or at night. The dor- sal, caudal and anal fins lie at the end of the body in close proximity and provide the thrust when the Pike pounces on prey. Pike live almost exclusively on fish. The Pike attains a length of up to 1.5 m and can weigh over 20 kg (excep- tionally up to 35 kg).

The Pike's colouring varies with the

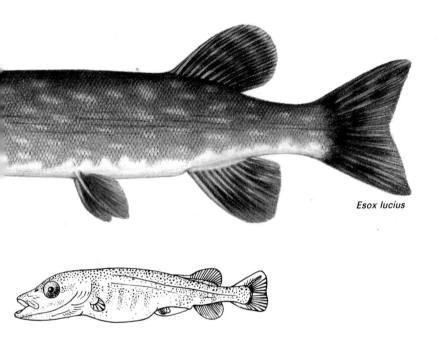

Esox lucius

Stages in development of *E. lucius*

environmental conditions. Young specimens are usually light green, brownish
or silvery. The dark spots on their sides
often merge to form cross-bands. Adult
pike have a dark green back, greenish
blue (and frequently yellow-spotted)
sides and a white belly. Their paired fins
are light-coloured and their unpaired
fins are marked with dark cross-stripes;
reddish or russet stripes can sometimes
be seen between the rays of the anal
and caudal fin.

The Pike is distributed over the whole
of Europe with the exception of the Iberian peninsula, the southern part of Italy
and the southern Balkans. It normally
frequents slow-flowing and stagnant
water, but often swims long distances
against the current from the lowland
reaches of rivers to the trout zone. Pike
spawn early in the spring, in March and
April, when they assemble in overgrown
shallows, old backwaters and flooded
meadows. The tiny eggs are stuck to
aquatic plants or grasses and the young
are hatched in 12—15 days.

In many places it is bred by artificial
spawning and is then transferred to
ponds and to open water, sometimes as
the newly hatched fry and sometimes—
preferably—when it is a little older. The
Pike is also very popular with anglers,
who catch it with a live or a dead fish
bait, a spoon lure or by spinning.

Distribution of *U. krameri*

Mudminnow
Umbra krameri Walbaum

The Mudminnow is a small, reddish brown, irregularly dark-spotted fish with a rounded caudal fin and a light band along its sides. There are scales on both the top and sides of its head. Its dorsal and anal fin are situated well back on its body and its ventral fins start from a point which is either perpendicularly below the anterior edge of the dorsal fin, or just in front of it. Its body and head are irregularly strewn with small dark spots and even its caudal and dorsal fin are spotted. The Mudminnow usually measures 5—10 cm (exceptionally up to 13 cm).

The Mudminnow is ancestrally related to the Pike, as testified by the relatively posterior positions of the dorsal and the anal fins and by recent palaeontological studies. Palaeontologists have demonstrated that the Tertiary forebears of Pike and Mudminnows split up into two separate branches as a result of differences in their mode of life. Pike became exclusively predatory, their bodies became larger and longer and the size of their mouth and recurved teeth increased. In the course of evolution their bodies acquired the typical dart-like form, while the dorsal and anal fin shifted right to the end of the body. Mudminnows, on the other hand, became adapted to a life in quiet water with abundant vegetation. Their body grew shorter, the dorsal and anal fin shifted a bit forwards, the tiny mouth with small teeth adapted to catching small creatures. In the Pike, the lateral line underwent marked development and divided into several lines branching to numerous pores on the head and jaws; the Mudminnow, however, has only a faint, light-coloured lateral line with no typical pores in the scales.

The Mudminnow lives in shallow water warmed by the sun, or in sluggish water with dense aquatic vegetation. It occurs in the Danube, from its middle reaches in Austria as far as the delta, in Lake Balaton and in the rivers Prut and Dnestr. It lives mainly on aquatic crustaceans and insect larvae, and imagos which fall on to the surface of the water. The Mudminnow is a typical short-lived fish, with a life span of only three (exceptionally five) years. It prepares a nest for the eggs and spawns at water temperatures of 12—18 °C. The female defends the fertilized eggs and the newly hatched fry.

Umbra krameri

Umbra pygmaea

This small and comparatively rare little fish is not economically important. Modern land improvement and water construction works have led to a rapid decrease in the number of places suitable for its successful development, with the result that the Mudminnow is now included among the seriously en-dangered and protected fish species. Its North American relative the Eastern Mudminnow, *Umbra pygmaea* (De Kay) has been imported into Europe several times by aquarists and is often kept in ornamental pools and ponds. Both species are only occasionally kept in aquaria.

Distribution of *R. rutilus*

Distribution of *R. rubilio*

Roach
Rutilus rutilus (L.)

○ ■
Cyprinid fishes
Cyprinidae

The Roach is a member of the carp family with relatively large scales firmly embedded in its skin. It has a dark brown or grey back with a bluish or greenish lustre, silvery white sides and a white, rounded belly. Its dorsal and caudal fin are grey; the other fins are reddish. It has a terminal mouth and red eyes. Roach living in different types of water have different forms; in water with too little food and too many fish they are relatively long and slender, while in water with a good food supply their body is shorter and relatively high.

The Roach is one of the commonest European fishes to be found in all types of water—ponds, rivers, streams, lakes and dams. It is distributed over the whole of Europe from England and France north of the Alps to the Urals in the east and from there into Asia; it does not occur in Portugal, Spain and Italy, on the Adriatic coast of Yugoslavia, or in Albania and Greece. In Scandinavia its range stretches from the south of Norway across Sweden but it does not occur in the western part of Norway. It often invades brackish water and it also lives in the Baltic, where it is a migratory anadromous fish. As a rule it measures about 25 cm and weighs 250—400 g, but in exceptional cases can

measure over 35 cm and weigh about 1 kg. It lives in large shoals.

In April and May it spawns in shallow water among aquatic plants. The males are conspicuous for their spawning rash. The fertilized eggs are stuck to the vegetation and the fry hatch in about 12 days. Under natural conditions Roach often interbreed with other cyprinid fishes (Common Bream, Bleak or Rudd). The young live mainly on planktonic and benthic invertebrate animals, while aquatic plants and detritus form a substantial part of the diet of the adults; insect larvae and imagos play only a minor role.

In some places the Roach is an economically very important fish in lakes, large dams, ponds and rivers. It is caught with dragnets, seines, drop-nets and gill nets. It is popular with anglers, both as a catch and as bait for angling predators.

In Italy, the Roach is replaced by the related *Rutilus rubilio* Bonaparte, which can also be encountered in Yugoslavian, Albanian and Greek rivers emptying into the Adriatic and the Mediterranean. Separate subspecies live in lakes Ohrid and Prespa in Macedonia. On the Iberian Peninsula, the Roach is represented by several species described by Stein-

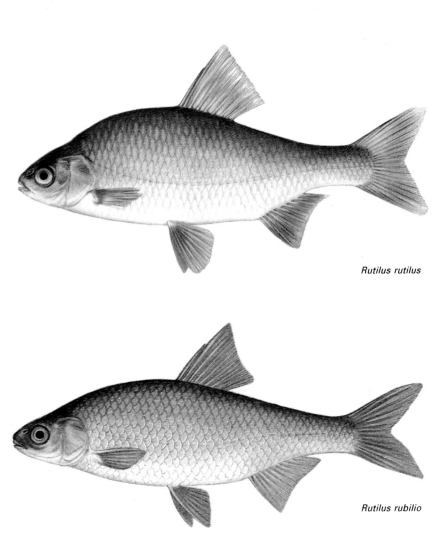

Rutilus rutilus

Rutilus rubilio

dachner; *R. arcasii, R. lemmingii, R. alburnoides* and *R. macrolepidotus* live in the western part. Another species, *R. macedonicus* (Steindachner), occurs in the river Vardar in the Balkans. These species are all of only limited local economic significance.

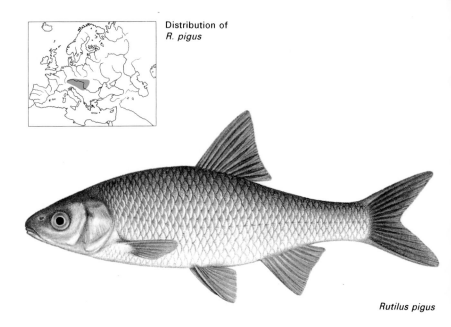

Rutilus pigus

Danubian Roach
Rutilus pigus (Lacépède)

Cyprinid fishes
Cyprinidae

The Danubian Roach is a cyprinid fish inhabiting deep water. It can be distinguished from the Roach by the larger number of scales in its lateral line, the dark lining of its abdominal cavity and its colouring in general; its opercula and sides have an opalescent sheen (which is especially marked in the spawning season), its dorsal fin is reddish and its caudal fin is yellowish red. It has relatively large scales and a ventral mouth. The Danubian Roach can be up to 50 cm long and weigh 1.5—2 kg and is thus larger than the Roach.

The subspecies *R. p. pigus* lives in the Alpine lakes Maggiore, Lugano, Como and Garda in northern Italy, in the basin of the River Po and in a number of smaller rivers. It inhabits deep water near the river bed. The only time it oc-

curs in shallow water is at spawning time, in April and May, when the males have a conspicuous spawning rash on their head and sides and, like the females, are very strikingly coloured. This species feeds mainly on benthos.

The subspecies *R. p. virgo* (Heckel), occurs in the upper and middle reaches of the Danube and in its tributaries. It has an elongate, flat-sided body, a grey-green back, blue-gleaming sides and a white, faintly bluish belly. It frequents deep water and lives on benthic invertebrates.

The small cyprinid fishes belonging to the genera *Phoxinellus* and *Paraphoxinus* are considered to be closely akin to the Roach. Two species have already been mentioned in association with the salmonid fishes *Salmo letnica* and *Sal-*

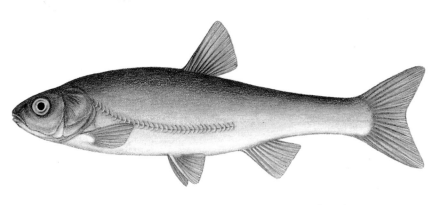

Paraphoxinus alepidotus

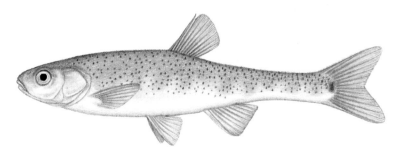

Paraphoxinus ghethaldii

mothymus ohridianus in Lake Ohrid in Macedonia. The slim, slightly flat-sided Spanish Minnow carp, *Phoxinellus hispanicus* (Steindachner) lives in southwestern Spain, in small rivers in the basin of the river Guadiana, where it forms shoals near the surface of the water. Six small members of the genus *Paraphoxinus* are to be found in various parts of Yugoslavia; *P. alepidotus* and *P. adspersus* (described by Heckel) occur in Dalmatia and Steindachner's *P. croaticus*, *P. ghethaldii*, *P. pstrossi* and *P. epiroticus* elsewhere along the eastern shores of the Adriatic. *P. ghethaldii* is a particularly interesting little fish. Like the others, it measures about 10 cm, but it inhabits the water in caves in the karst region of Bosnia and Herzegovina. Living as it does in the dark, it is very characteristically coloured; it has a dingy brown back, yellowish to golden yellow sides and a white belly, while the whole of its body is thinly speckled with small, irregular brownish black spots. It lives mainly on underground aquatic crustaceans. The other *Paraphoxinus* species live above ground in fresh water and are normally coloured, with a dark greenish or brownish back, lighter sides (often spotted or striped) and a white belly. Their form and habits are reminiscent of the Minnow, a familiar inhabitant of streams and small rivers in western, central and eastern Europe.

Distribution of *R. frisii*

Black Sea Roach; Pearl Roach
Rutilus frisii (NORDMANN)

● ○ ■
Cyprinid fishes
Cyprinidae

This large roach from the Black Sea region usually grows to a length of 40—50 cm and weighs about 1—1.5 kg, although in exceptional cases it may measure 70 cm and weigh up to 7 kg. It has a long, cylindrical, only slightly flat-sided body and the root of its tail is relatively thin and long—a mark of an expert swimmer. Its mouth is small and situated ventrally. The Black Sea Roach has relatively small scales, smaller than those of other roaches. It has a brownish black, green-tinted back and silvery sides changing over gradually to a white belly. Its fins are all transparent and are grey, faintly tinged with yellow or orange (especially the anal and dorsal fin). Its eyes have a yellow to brick red iris.

The Black Sea Roach is a migratory fish which normally inhabits brackish water, but in the spawning season, in March and April, it migrates far up the rivers on the north and east side of the Black Sea (the Dnestr, Bug, Dnepr and Don, etc). The eggs are deposited in sand and among aquatic plants. The fish seldom take food while migrating, but in brackish water they live chiefly on worms, molluscs and various crustaceans. They are sexually mature by their fourth or fifth year. The nominate subspecies, *R. f. frisii*, is an economically

important fish in the Black Sea region. It is caught with different types of nets, mostly while journeying upstream.

Three more subspecies occur in other parts of Europe. *R. f. meidingeri* lives in Alpine lakes belonging to the Danubian system (the Chiemsee, Traunsee, Attersee and Mondsee). It spawns in the tributary streams and rivers of these lakes, usually in April and May, when the males have a strikingly red belly. In addition to various invertebrates, this subspecies catches small fish. It is of considerable local significance, both economically (it is caught with nets in the rivers above the lakes while migrating) and for anglers, who mostly fish on the bottom for it.

From time to time, this subspecies leaves its Alpine lakes and infiltrates the upper reaches of the Danube; in 1975 a specimen was caught in the Slovakian stretch of the Danube, not far from Bratislava.

Another subspecies, *R. f. velecensis*, lives in the east of Bulgaria, in the rivers Veleka and Rezova. *R. f. kutum* inhabits the southern parts of the Caspian Sea and its tributary rivers: this is an important fish for Caspian fishermen, who catch it both in brackish water and also in the rivers, while it is migrating.

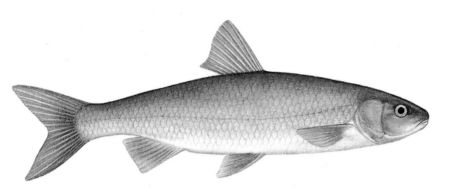

Rutilus frisii — a form living in streams and rivers

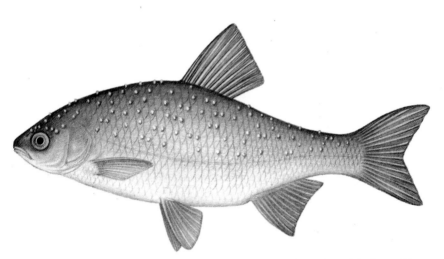

Rutilus frisii meidingeri — a lake form with spawning rash

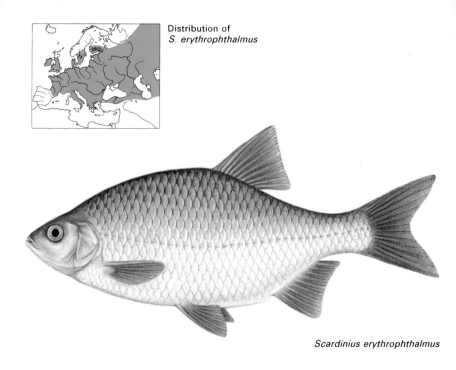

Distribution of
S. erythrophthalmus

Scardinius erythrophthalmus

Rudd
Scardinius erythrophthalmus (L.)

Cyprinid fishes
Cyprinidae

At first glance the Rudd looks very much like the Roach, but on its belly, behind its ventral fins, it has a sharp-edged keel covered with scales, while here the Roach's belly is rounded. The Rudd's dorsal fin is situated further back than the Roach's and begins from the end of an imaginary line perpendicular to the base of the ventral fins. The Rudd has a flat-sided body and its small, terminal mouth curves obliquely upwards. It has a bluish green back and its sides and belly are silvery white. Its dorsal fin and pectoral fins are grey, tinged with red; its other fins are all bright red. As distinct from the red-eyed Roach, the Rudd has yellow to orange irises. The Rudd usually mea-sures 25—30 cm and weighs about 250 g, but may occasionally be up to 40 cm long and weigh about 1 kg.

The Rudd is distributed over the whole of Europe except the Iberian peninsula, Scotland, the northern parts of Scandinavia, the Crimea and the south of Greece. The subspecies *S. e. scarda-fa* occurs in middle and southern Italy, northern Dalmatia and the basins of the rivers Vardar, Struma, Mesta and Mari-tza in Bulgaria and Yugoslavia.

Rudd inhabit stagnant and sluggish water thickly overgrown with aquatic vegetation. They live in small shoals, often near the surface and close to the edge. They spawn in May and June and are typically phytophilous fish. Up to

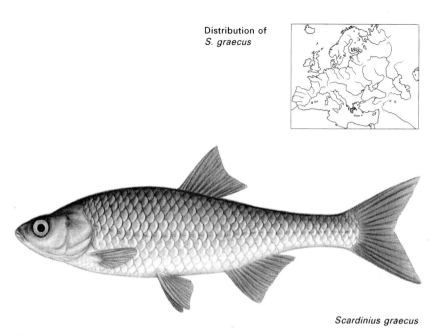

Scardinius graecus

a length of about 7 cm their food consists of plankton; later they live mainly on aquatic plants. The Rudd's economic significance is negligible.

In warm thermal springs near the town of Oradea in north-west Romania lives a small fish not more than 9 cm long, which some authors regard as a subspecies of the Rudd and others as a separate species, *Scardinius rakovitzai* Müller. The springs have a temperature of 28—34 °C and in the course of the ages the fish has become so used to the warmth that in water with a temperature of less than 20 °C it dies. It spawns at the age of one, or at most two, years, from the end of February to the middle of March, and dies soon af-

ter spawning. Its form and colouring are different from those of the Rudd living in normal water; it has a low body with thicker sides and a longer head, a green back, golden-yellow sides and a light yellow belly.

A further species, *S. graecus* Stephanidis, occurs in the south of Greece. This fish has a long, flat-sided body and the top of its head appears to have been dented; it measures up to 40 cm. Like the Rudd, it lives in shoals and its food consists mainly of small crustaceans, insect larvae and flying insects, although it also eats aquatic plants. It is of little and only local economic significance.

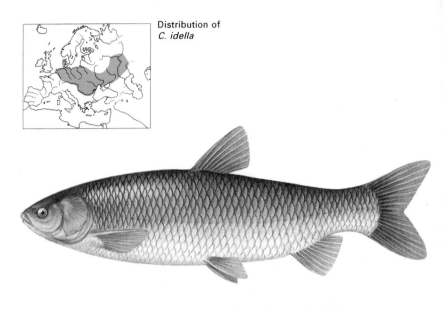

Distribution of
C. idella

Ctenopharyngodon idella

Grass Carp
Ctenopharyngodon idella (V<small>ALENCIENNES</small>)

During the past few decades, several cyprinid fishes from the Far East have been introduced into European waters, mainly to consume aquatic plants despised by native species. The first of these 'foreigners', the Grass Carp, is a large cyprinid fish from the middle and lower reaches of the river Amur and from China. It has a long, mildly flat-sided body covered with large scales, a very wide head with a semi-ventral mouth and pronounced radial grooves on its opercula. It is coloured similarly to the Wild Carp, but its sides are a little lighter and have a golden lustre. The Grass Carp grows to a length of well over 1 m and can weigh more than 30 kg; it grows very fast. In China, south of Canton, it has been kept in ponds since time immemorial and since 1950 it

has been 'on trial' in ponds in the European part of the USSR and subsequently in other European countries as well.

The Grass Carp normally lives on aquatic plants, but in ponds it will also accept various fodder plants, such as lucerne and clover, etc. It is sexually mature at 5—8 years and spawns from April onwards, right through the summer, in the current of large rivers when the temperature rises to 15—18 °C. The eggs are pelagic, i.e. they float freely in the water and are carried along by the current. The fry collect in quiet water near the bank, in old creeks and in similar peaceful spots. Under European conditions, spawning is carried out artificially in June and July. The Grass Carp is a promising fish, especially for warm European fishpond regions.

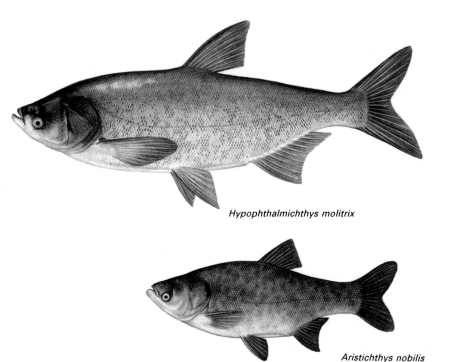

Hypophthalmichthys molitrix

Aristichthys nobilis

Silver Carp
Hypophthalmichthys molitrix (Valenciennes)

○ □
Cyprinid fishes
Cyprinidae

The Silver Carp, another cyprinid fish which has been introduced into Europe from the Far East, lives on plankton in general and on unicellular green and blue-green algae in particular. It has a robust, thick-set body covered with tiny scales, a large, wide head and a distinctly dorsal mouth. Its lower jaw projects beyond the upper jaw and its eyes are situated unusually low down on the head. A sharp, scaleless keel runs down the middle of its belly. Its head and back are greyish green; its sides and belly are silvery.

The Silver Carp lives in stagnant and sluggish water with an adequate supply of plankton. It grows quickly and, under European conditions, weighs 1.5—2 kg by the time it is 3—4 years old; it is sexually mature at 5—6 years.

Its establishment in European ponds and in some reservoirs threatened by the overproliferation of phytoplankton has so far been successful, but unfortunately for anglers it is a difficult fish to catch with rod and line.

Attempts to introduce the related *Aristichthys nobilis* (Richardson) have been less successful. This fish, which comes from China, lives mainly on zooplankton, but in ponds it can also be fed on the same food as carp. Although it grows very quickly, it is still bred only on a limited scale in European ponds.

Distribution of
L. cephalus

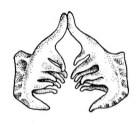

Pharyngeal teeth of *L. cephalus*

Chub
Leuciscus cephalus (L.)

○ ■
Cyprinid fishes
Cyprinidae

The most widespread European member of the genus *Leuciscus* is undoubtedly the Chub, which occurs over the whole of Europe with the exception of Ireland, Denmark, the north of Scandinavia and the European part of the USSR. It has a long, cylindrical body with large grey- or black-bordered scales making a dark network pattern all over it. Its back is greyish brown tinged with green, its sides are lighter and often golden and its belly is white. Its dorsal and caudal fin are greyish green, frequently with a touch of red, and its anal fin and ventral fins are orange-red. It has a large, wide mouth. It differs from the related and similar Dace in respect of its large mouth, the arrangement of the pharyngeal teeth and the shape of the anal fin, which is concave in the Dace and convex in the Chub. The Chub generally measures 40—50 cm and weighs 2—3 kg, but occasionally more.

Young Chubs live together in shoals; older fish live solitarily. The Chub lives in both flowing and stagnant water and is also to be encountered in brackish water in river mouths. It prefers a hard bed and in rivers will often swim upstream into the trout zone, where it is an unwelcome guest, since it competes with the trout for food and is a danger to the young. Small invertebrates form the staple diet of young Chub, but later on they live mainly on small fish and other small vertebrates. They also like fruit—a useful piece of knowledge for anglers.

The Chub spawns among aquatic plants and on stones in swift, turbulent parts of the rivers from April to June, when the males are covered with a spawning rash. At temperatures of about 15 °C, the fry hatch in roughly four days.

The Chub is an important fish in water where there are no trout. It is caught with nets or is angled in a variety of ways—by spinning, with live bait, with dead bait and by fly-fishing.

In addition to the typical Chub, several subspecies live in Europe. *L. c. albus* is to be found from the middle of Italy and across Dalmatia to the Peloponnese peninsula, *L. cephalus cabeda* occurs in the north of Italy and the south of France, *L. c. macedonicus* is distributed throughout the basins of the

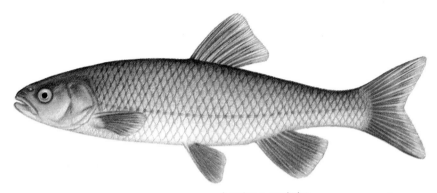

Leuciscus cephalus

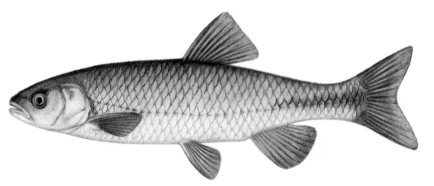

Leuciscus borysthenicus

rivers Struma, Mesta and Maritza in the Balkans, *L. pyrenaicus* lives in Spain and Portugal and the still somewhat doubtful subspecies *L. cephalus vardarensis* has been described from the catchment area of the river Vardar in the east of the Yugoslavian part of Macedonia.

The small species *L. illyricus* (Heckel et Kner), which measures only 25 cm, is known from the Dalmatian rivers Kerka and Cetina. Another *Leuciscus* species, *L. borysthenicus* (Kessler), lives in rivers flowing into the Black Sea from the east of Bulgaria to Transcaucasia, while the tiny *L. aphipsi* Aleksandrov inhabits the tributaries of the lower reaches of the river Kuban (USSR).

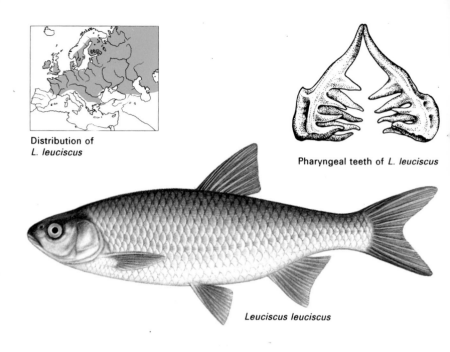

Distribution of
L. leuciscus

Pharyngeal teeth of *L. leuciscus*

Leuciscus leuciscus

Dace
Leuciscus leuciscus (L.)

■
Cyprinid fishes
Cyprinidae

The commonest of the smaller members of this genus in Europe is the Dace, which has a long, and in cross section almost completely round body. The back is dark grey to black with a touch of blue and it has silvery sides and a white belly. It is distinguished from the larger Chub by its concave anal fin. It measures maximally 35 cm and weighs about 250 g.

The Dace forms shoals in the fast parts of clean submontane and lowland rivers and streams. It lives on larval and adult insects, which it gathers from the surface of the water. It spawns among aquatic plants in flowing water from March to May; in the spawning season the males have a spawning rash on their head and body.

The Dace occurs over the whole of Europe with the exception of the three southern peninsulas, Scotland and the northern part of Scandinavia. In some places it is caught with nets; anglers like to fish for it with artificial flies. A separate subspecies, *L. l. burdigalensis*, lives in the south of France.

Further small species of the same genus include *L. danilewski* (Kessler), which occurs in the Don and Dnestr basins, *L. svallize* (Heckel et Kner) in Dalmatian and Albanian rivers and the Croatian species *L. polylepis* (Steindachner), all of which grow to a length of about 20—25 cm.

Distribution of *L. souffia*

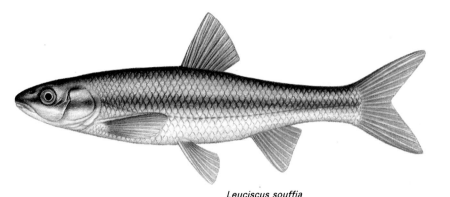

Leuciscus souffia

Souffie
Leuciscus souffia RISSO

Cyprinid fishes
Cyprinidae

The Souffie is a small cyprinid fish with a long, cylindrical body and a ventral mouth. A wide dark band runs the full length of its silvery sides and below it, especially in the spawning season, we can see the orange-red canals of the lateral line. The Souffie occurs in the basins of the Rhône and the Var in the south of France. The subspecies *L. s. agassizi* lives in the catchment area of the upper Rhine and the upper and middle Danube, while *L. s. muticellus* lives in northern and central Italy.

The Souffie lives in shoals and prefers the deeper parts of streams and rivers. It spawns in stony places, in flow-

ing water, and both sexes have a spawning rash. Its diet consists of small aquatic invertebrate animals and of insects which fall on to the surface of the water.

Other small members of the genus, as well as the Souffie, have long dark side stripes leading from the eyes to the root of the tail. They include *L. ukliva* (Heckel) in the river Cetina in Dalmatia, *L. microlepis* (Heckel) in the Neretva and *L. turskyi* (Heckel), which likewise lives in Dalmatia, in the rivers Cicola and Narenta. Like the Souffie, these fish all grow to a length of about 25 cm and have similar habits.

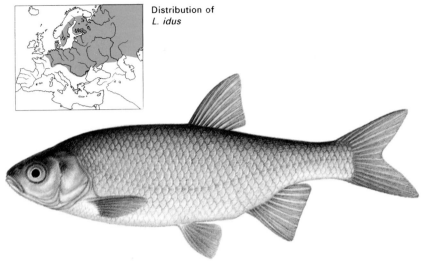

Distribution of
L. idus

Leuciscus idus

Ide
Leuciscus idus (L.)

○ ■
Cyprinid fishes
Cyprinidae

The Ide normally measures 40—50 cm and weighs about 2 kg, although specimens up to 80 cm long and weighing about 5 kg have occasionally been caught. The Ide has a relatively deep, somewhat flat-sided body, a rather small head with a neat little mouth and quite large eyes. Its back is greyish blue to blackish green, its sides are silvery and its belly is white. The dorsal, caudal and anal fins are grey, the others are yellowish to reddish; the caudal fin is deeply forked.

In Europe, the Ide's distribution area stretches from the Rhine to the Ural and from there into Asia; it does not occur in the British Isles, in France, in the south European peninsulas or in the north of Scandinavia.

The Ide frequents the lower reaches of large rivers from the barbel zone to the brackish water in their estuaries. It forms shoals and favours the upper layers of the water. It lives on zooplankton and benthic animals (midge and other insect larvae, worms, aquatic molluscs, etc.) and small fish. Its life span is generally 10—15 years. It is sexually mature at three to five years, when it measures 20—30 cm. In the spring it migrates upstream to places with a sandy or gravelly bed and sometimes with abundant aquatic vegetation, where it spawns from April to June. The eggs are stuck to the bottom or to aquatic plants. In the spawning season male ides are covered with a spawning rash.

In some regions (e.g. in the Danube basin) the Ide is economically quite important. It is caught with different types of nets—wicker traps, drop-nets, gill nets and dragnets. It is also very popular with anglers, who use dead bait and artificial flies. In addition to the nominate form, a subspecies, *L. i. stagnalis*, occurs in south-western Europe.

Leuciscus idus aberr. *orfus*

Orfe
Leuciscus idus aberr. *orfus* (L.)

Cyprinid fishes
Cyprinidae

This golden form of the Ide is often kept as a decorative fish in carp ponds. Its body is orange to reddish, fading away to white on the belly. The Orfe is also kept in ponds in gardens and parks, frequently together with goldfish. It requires much more oxygen in the water than goldfish, however, and is therefore more difficult to keep and especially to breed.

Minnow
Phoxinus phoxinus (L.)

Cyprinid fishes
Cyprinidae

The Minnow is a tiny fish seldom more than 6—10 cm long, with very small scales and frequently with an incomplete lateral line. It has a tiny terminal mouth and relatively large eyes. Down its brownish green back runs a row of dark spots, which often unite to form a longitudinal band; sometimes, however, they form dark cross stripes extending below the lateral line. In the spawning season the males are gaudily coloured; they have a very dark back, golden sides and a red belly and the edge of their lips and the base of their paired fins and anal fin are also red. The females are more soberly coloured, but they also have a spawning rash like the males.

In Europe, the Minnow's range stretches eastwards from the north of Spain and northern Italy; it does not include the more northern parts of Scandinavia, the north of Scotland, the southern parts of the Iberian peninsula, middle and southern Italy and the Peloponnese. Most of the Minnow's territory is occupied by the nominate subspecies, but from Novorossiisk to Batumi in the USSR it is occupied by the Transcaucasian subspecies *P. p. colchicus*.

The Minnow lives in shoals in clean streams and mountain rivers with a sandy or stony bed at altitudes of up to 2,000 m; it is often to be found in the trout zone and in some places it occurs in clean lakes. Minnows are a very sensitive biological indicator of the cleanness and oxygen content of the water. Their diet consists of small benthic invertebrate animals and insects. If alarmed, they disappear like a flash under stones or an overhanging bank. In the spawning season, from April to June, they migrate short distances to sandy stretches of their streams and rivers, where they spawn in shallow water on the bed. Lake populations generally spawn in the tributary rivers of the lake. In trout streams, these tiny, lively little cyprinid fish are frequently an important component of the diet of the economically valuable Brown Trout.

The related Swamp Minnow, *P. percnurus* (Pallas), occurs in the catchment areas of the Oder and the Vistula, in eastern Europe and in Asia. It is not so slender as the Minnow and has a dark brown, green-tinted back, yellowish brown sides irregularly speckled with dark spots and a white belly. Unlike the Minnow, it lives in stagnant water with dense aquatic vegetation; its oxygen requirements are much less exacting. Its eggs are deposited on aquatic plants.

The nominate form of *P. percnurus* inhabits the rivers flowing into the Arctic Ocean, from the N. Dvina eastwards as far as the river Kolyma, and three subspecies live in the Vistula and Oder basins — *P. p. dybowskii* in the Warsaw region, *P. p. gdaniensis* in the area round Gdansk and *P. p. posnaniensis* in the Poznan area. The subspecies *P. p. stagnalis* occurs in lakes along the middle reaches of the Volga.

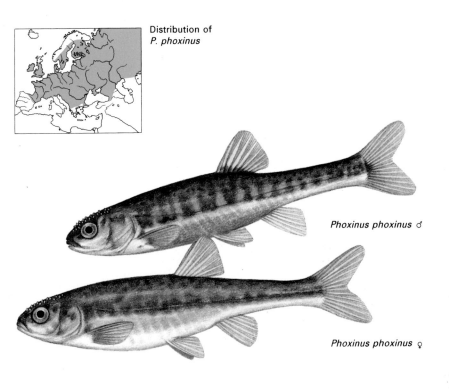

Distribution of
P. phoxinus

Phoxinus phoxinus ♂

Phoxinus phoxinus ♀

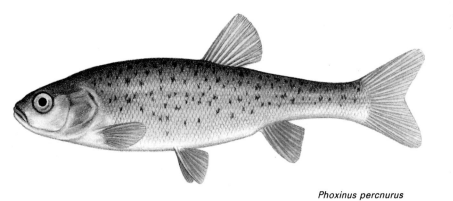

Phoxinus percnurus

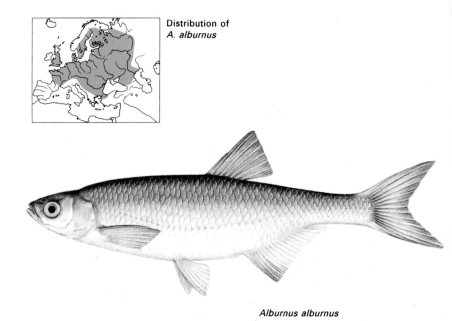

Distribution of
A. alburnus

Alburnus alburnus

Bleak
Alburnus alburnus (L.)

►
Cyprinid fishes
Cyprinidae

The Bleak is a long, slender, flat-sided cyprinid fish with an almost straight back and a small, typically superior mouth. Between its ventral fins and its anal fin there is a sharp-edged, scaleless keel. Its body is covered with relatively large, loose scales. The Bleak has a greyish green or greyish blue back, silvery gleaming sides and a white belly. Its dorsal and caudal fin are greyish, with a yellow base; the other fins are pale yellow; there are 18—23 rays in its anal fin.

The Bleak inhabits Europe north of the Pyrenees and the Alps as far as the Urals; it does not occur in Ireland and Scotland, the Iberian peninsula, Italy, the western part of the Balkans, the Crimea and the northern part of Scandi-

navia. Two subspecies live in southern Europe — *A. a. macedonicus* in the basin of the river Vardar in Yugoslavia and *A. a. strumicae* in the catchment area of the rivers Struma and Mesta in Bulgaria.

Bleak are typical fish of slow-flowing and stagnant water. During the daytime they remain near the surface, eating insects which have fallen on to the water, insect larvae and zooplankton, but at night they retire to deeper water. They have an average life span of three to six years and grow to a length of 17—20 cm. They spawn in shoals in May and June, generally on the aquatic vegetation, but often on stones, gravel and other substrates. In the spawning season the males have striking spawning

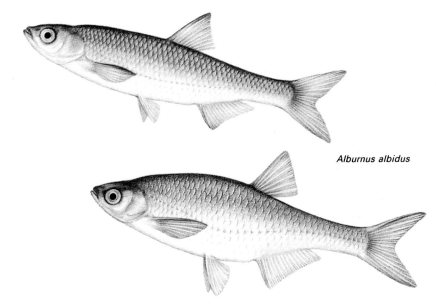

Alburnus albidus

Alburnus charusini

tubercles. Like many other cyprinid fishes, the Bleak spawns intermittently, at intervals of about 10—14 days.

The south Italian species the White Bleak, *A. albidus*, which is closely related to the Bleak, has fewer rays (14—16) in its anal fin; its colouring and habits are similar to those of the preceding species, however. The nominate form lives only in the southern half of Italy; in the northern part, in Dalmatia and in lakes Shkodër (Scutari) and Ohrid its place is taken by the subspecies *A. a. alborella*. The subspecies *A. a. belvica* reportedly lives in Lake Prespa and *A. a. scoranzoides* in waters in Montenegro (Yugoslavia).

Another species, *A. charusini* Herzenstein, has a higher, extremely flat-sided body and its tail is strikingly thin at the root. It lives in shoals in lakes associated with the lower reaches of the Volga, the Ural, the Terek and the Kuban.

The Bleak is of only local economic importance; in some places, for instance in Lake Ohrid in Macedonia, it is popular with anglers. It is caught for human consumption mainly in the autumn; otherwise it is fished for fodder (fish meal). The scales of Bleak from Lake Ohrid are important raw material for making imitation pearls, the manufacture of which is a close-kept secret. Lastly, all *Alburnus* species are frequently employed as bait for catching predators.

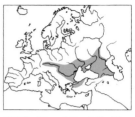

Distribution of *C. chalcoides*

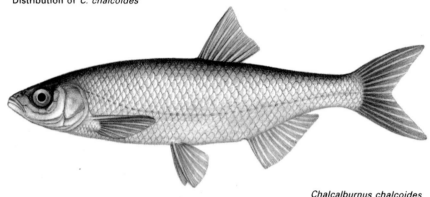

Chalcalburnus chalcoides

Shemaya; Danubian Bleak
Chalcalburnus chalcoides (GÜLDENSTÄDT)

● ○
Cyprinid fishes
Cyprinidae

This slender, flat-sided cyprinid fish has a long body and a distinctive dorsal mouth; its lower jaw projects beyond the upper jaw. On its belly, behind its ventral fins, it has a scaleless keel. Its back is blackish green, its sides are silvery and its belly is white. The dorsal fin is situated a long way posteriorly and arises behind the ventral fins. Like the caudal fin it is dark grey; the other fins are lighter. The Shemaya grows to a length of 40 cm.

This anadromous fish lives in shoals in the Caspian Sea and the Black Sea. In the autumn it swims upstream, but does not spawn until May. It lives on benthos and flying insects. Several

permanently freshwater subspecies are known. *C. c. derjugini* lives in Crimean rivers flowing into the northern part of the Black Sea, *C. c. mandrensis* inhabits Lake Mandra in Bulgaria and *C. c. mento* is a resident freshwater form occurring in the Danube, the Alpine lakes of the Danubian system, small Bulgarian rivers emptying into the Black Sea and the Bug, Dnestr, Dnepr, Don and Kuban in the USSR.

The economic importance of this species increases in an eastward direction and in the region of the Caspian Sea it is an important fish for human consumption.

A detail of the lateral line of *A. bipunctatus*

Distribution of
A. bipunctatus

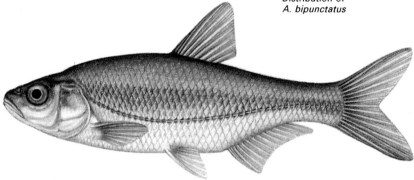

Alburnoides bipunctatus

Riffle Minnow; Schneider
Alburnoides bipunctatus (Bloch)

Cyprinid fishes
Cyprinidae

Although similar to the Bleak, the Riffle Minnow has a deeper body and on its sides, along the lateral line, runs a narrow, dark double stripe, with a further, wider dark stripe below it. The latter is sometimes less noticeable, but at spawning time is very pronounced. The ventral mouth is less strikingly uptilted than in the two preceding species. The Riffle Minnow has a greenish or greyish green back, silvery opalescent sides and a white belly. Its dorsal, caudal and pectoral fins are grey; its yellowish ventral fins and anal fin are deep orange at the base. It grows to a length of 10—15 cm.

In Europe it is to be found eastwards from France as far as the tributary rivers of the Caspian Sea; it does not occur in the Iberian peninsula, Italy, the western part of the Balkans, England, Denmark and northern Europe. Several subspecies, whose systematic status is still undecided, have been described in Bulgarian rivers, Lake Ohrid and the European part of the USSR.

The Riffle Minnow chiefly frequents shallow flowing water in the middle of the current. It spawns in May and June on a hard gravelly or sandy bed. It lives on the larvae of aquatic insects, aquatic crustaceans and insects floating on the surface. It has high oxygen requirements and as it does not tolerate water polluted by industrial, agricultural or urban waste it is a good biological indicator of the quality of the environment. Although economically unimportant, in some places it is used by anglers as bait.

101

Distribution of *L. delineatus*

Moderlieschen; Belica
Leucaspius delineatus (HECKEL)

▶
Cyprinid fishes
Cyprinidae

The Moderlieschen is one of the smallest European freshwater fishes and adult specimens usually measure only 5—7 cm (occasionally up to 9 cm). It has a slim, flat-sided body covered with loose scales. Its lateral line is incomplete and can be seen on not more than the first 12 scales. Its back is usually olive green, while its sides and belly are silvery, with a metallic blue lustre. Its fins are dull grey, sometimes tinged with red.

In Europe the Moderlieschen is distributed eastwards from the Rhine and its tributaries as far as the Caspian Sea. It does not occur on the British Isles or in France, Switzerland, the Iberian peninsula, Italy south of the Alps or the Balkans and in Scandinavia it lives only in the southernmost parts of Sweden.

The Moderlieschen forms large shoals in slow-flowing and stagnant water thickly overgrown with aquatic vegetation; in some places it is also very common in fishponds and their connecting canals, in backwaters, in irrigation canals and in river arms.

It spawns in April and May among aquatic plants. The female lays the eggs in strings round the stems of the plants and the male, after fertilizing them, remains on guard. The males have a spawning rash, while the females have a conspicuous urogenital papilla

with three protuberances. The newly hatched fry are very active and form shoals just below the surface. Young Moderlieschen live mainly on planktonic unicellular algae, the older fish on zooplankton. In water free from predators, Moderlieschen sometimes multiply on an enormous scale, producing dwarf populations in which the adult fish do not measure more than 3—4 cm.

In some regions, Moderlieschen are caught with various types of nets and are pickled in oil and/or vinegar. Anglers also frequently use them as bait for catching predatory fish.

The related Tsima, *Leucaspius marathonicus* Vinciguerra, inhabits the area round Marathon in Greece; it forms shoals near the surface and lives on small planktonic crustaceans, insect larvae and winged insects gathered from the surface of the water. In Lake Stymphalia in the Peloponnese lives a similar fish which some ichthyologists consider to be a subspecies of *L. marathonicus* and others to be a separate species, *L. stymphalicus* (Cuvier et Valenciennes). The only difference between the two is the number of rays in the anal fin—14 in *L. marathonicus* and only 9—11 in *L. stymphalicus*. The biology of these two species is very similar to the biology of the Moderlieschen, but the south European species are somewhat larger.

Leucaspius delineatus

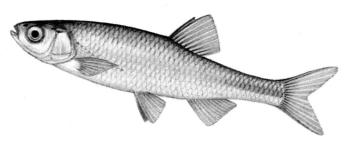

Leucaspius stymphalicus

103

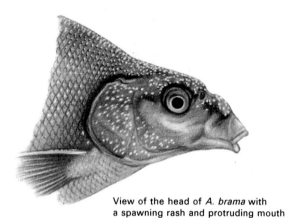

Distribution of
A. brama

View of the head of *A. brama* with
a spawning rash and protruding mouth

Common Bream
Abramis brama (L.)

○ ■
Cyprinid fishes
Cyprinidae

The Common Bream, the most wide-spread and most important representative of the genus *Abramis*, has a strikingly deep body with highly compressed sides and a distinctly inferior, protrusible mouth. Its dark back frequently has a greenish tinge, its sides are silvery grey and its belly is whitish. Young specimens are silvery, while old Bream are dark and often have a golden lustre on their sides. The fins are all greyish blue, but the unpaired fins are lighter than the paired fins. The scales are large and deciduous; between the ventral fins and the anus there is a scaleless keel.

In Europe, the Common Bream's distribution area stretches from England and the middle of France eastwards, north of the Alps, to the Urals and from there into Asia. It does not occur on the Iberian peninsula, in Italy, in the west of France, in the southern parts of the Balkans and in the Crimea and neither is it to be found in the north of Scotland or the western and northern parts of Scandinavia. In addition to the nominate

form, two further subspecies occur in Europe—*A. b. orientalis* in the region round the Caspian Sea and the Sea of Aral and *A. b. danubi* in the catchment area of the Danube.

The Common Bream is a gregarious fish of the lower reaches of large rivers, which are named the 'bream zone' after it. It forms large shoals, especially when young. It favours deep water with abundant vegetation, but looks for food in shallow water near the bank, especially in the evening and at night. It grows slowly and takes 7—8 years to attain a length of about 30 cm. On an average, a length of 30—40 cm and a weight of 1—2 kg are normal, but specimens weighing 3—5 kg are by no means rare. In some waters (especially dams), the Common Bream has multiplied so prolifically that the population is composed of stunted fish.

Young Common Bream live chiefly on zooplankton, older fish mainly on small benthic fauna, which they gather from the soft mud with their sensitive, tubularly protrusible mouth.

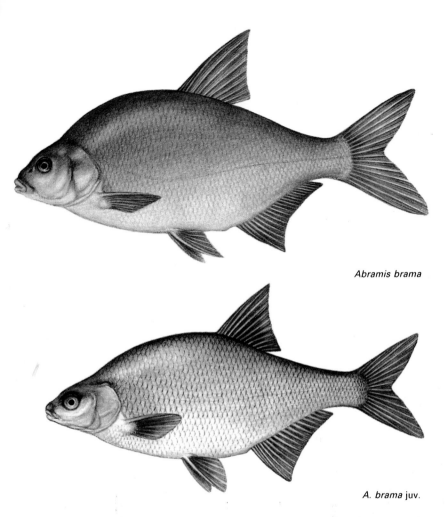

Abramis brama

A. brama juv.

The Common Bream becomes sexually mature at 4—7 years, but often lives to the ripe old age of 20—25 years. It spawns in large shoals in May and June, at water temperatures of 12—16 °C; the eggs are laid in two or three batches on water weeds and submerged plants in shallow water near the bank. If no actual plants are available, the fish spawn on submerged branches or brushwood, or on artificial redds made of sticks and branches attached to a floating wooden frame. In the spawning season, the male Common Bream has pronounced tubercles on its head, body and fins.

The Common Bream is a commercially important fish, especially in the more northern parts of Europe, where it is caught with dragnets, gill nets and drop-nets. In some places it is a popular fish with anglers, who catch it mostly on the bottom, using either plant or animal bait. Its flesh is very tasty and is suitable for smoking.

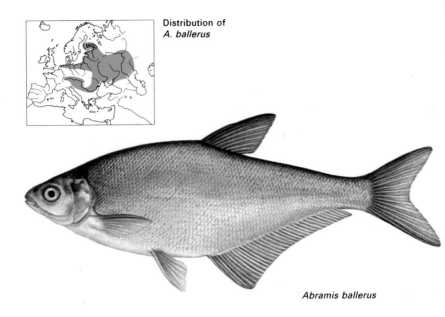

Abramis ballerus

Zope; Blue Bream
Abramis ballerus (L.)

Cyprinid fishes
Cyprinidae

The Zope is the slimmest of the European breams and has the narrowest body. Its extremely long anal fin is reinforced with three hard rays and 25—44 soft rays. Seen from the side it has a relatively pointed head and a terminal mouth sloping obliquely upwards. Its back is dark brown, with a greenish or bluish sheen, its sides are lighter and tinged with yellow and its belly is white. The Zope has greyish to faintly yellow, dark-edged fins. It grows to a length of up to 35 cm and weighs about 1 kg.

It inhabits the rivers flowing into the North Sea and the Baltic and the tributary rivers of the Black Sea, the Sea of Azov and the Caspian Sea. It occurs east of the Elbe as far as the Neva and in the Danube basin as far as Upper Austria and it also lives in the southern parts of Scandinavia and in the southeast as far as the basins of the Don, the Volga and the Ural in the USSR.

The Zope occurs in the lower reaches of rivers and in flood pools and lakes; it likes both slow-flowing and stagnant water. It forms small shoals and lives mainly on small zooplankton (in particular *Daphnia* and *Cyclops*), but also consumes a small amount of benthic fauna. It grows slowly and on an average reaches a length of about 30 cm by its eighth year; it attains sexual maturity at the age of three or four years. As a rule it spawns a little sooner than the Common Bream, from the second half of April to the end of May. The eggs are deposited on aquatic plants, on stones and on other submerged objects; the development of the embryos takes 4—5 days.

The Zope is economically important only in the eastern parts of Europe.

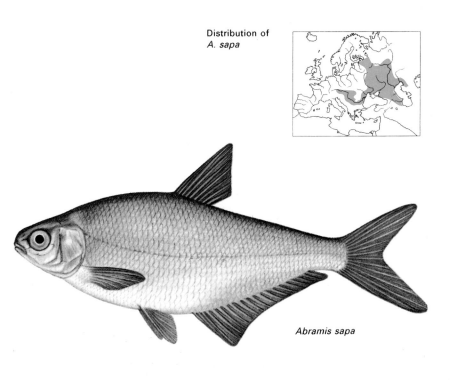

Abramis sapa

Danube Bream
Abramis sapa (PALLAS)

Cyprinid fishes
Cyprinidae

The Danube Bream has a similar form to the Zope and similarly has a long anal fin. However, it differs in respect of the ventral position of its mouth, the shape of its snout, the profile of the front of its body between the mouth and dorsal fin and its larger scales. Its eyes are strikingly large and the lower lobe of its caudal fin is longer than the upper lobe. The Danube Bream has a dark grey back tinged with green or blue, silvery grey sides and ash grey fins. It measures up to 30 cm and weighs about 0.5 kg. It inhabits the tributary rivers of the Black Sea, the Sea of Azov and the Caspian Sea from the Danube to the Ural.

The Danube Bream is not very common and frequents the lower reaches of big rivers, where it lives mainly on small benthic fauna. It is sexually mature at four years and usually spawns right in the course of the river on a gravelly bed. Prior to spawning it often undertakes long migrations, when the male is noticeable for the striking spawning rash on its head, body and inner surface of its pectoral and ventral fins. Spawning takes place in May and the fry hatch in four or five days.

The Danube Bream is not commercially important; its flesh is generally smoked.

107

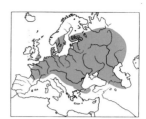

Distribution of
B. bjoerkna

Silver Bream; White Bream
Blicca bjoerkna (L.)

▶
Cyprinid fishes
Cyprinidae

At first glance the Silver Bream looks very much like the true breams of the genus *Abramis*, but can be distinguished from these without our having to examine its pharyngeal teeth, which are arranged in two rows (in true breams in one). The Silver Bream always has fewer than 50 scales in its lateral line—true breams always more. It likewise has fewer than 23 soft rays in its anal fin (true breams more) and there is also a difference in the number of soft rays in the dorsal fin (8 in the Silver Bream, 9—10 in true breams). Furthermore, the fins are differently coloured; in true breams the pectoral and ventral fins are greyish or dingy yellow, whereas in the Silver Bream they are always reddish or orange, at least at the base. Although the Silver Bream has a deep, flat-sided body, its sides are nevertheless more rounded and the fish as a whole is plumper. The Silver Bream's back is greyish blue or greyish green and in older fish is often very dark; its sides are gleaming silver and its belly is whitish, frequently tinged with pink. Its relatively large scales are firmly embedded in the skin. European Silver Bream usually measure about 20 cm and weigh up to 0.5 kg, although exceptionally they may be 30 cm long and weigh about 1 kg.

In Europe, the Silver Bream occurs north of the Pyrenees, the Alps and the Balkan Mountains (Stara Planina) in Bulgaria. From west to east its area stretches from eastern England and the basin of the Loire to the basin of the river Pechora in the USSR and it is also to be encountered in the southern parts of Scandinavia and the regions round the Black Sea and the Caspian Sea.

The Silver Bream is a common and in some places a very abundant fish in the lower reaches (bream zone) of rivers and in ponds, lakes and dams; it also abounds in old backwaters and in pools overgrown with water weeds. It forms shoals, which remain largely near the bed. When young, its diet consists mainly of planktonic organisms and algae; when adult, it contains a large proportion of various benthic invertebrates (particularly midge larvae) and sometimes aquatic plants. The Silver Bream reaches sexual maturity in its second or third year, but it grows very slowly and does not measure 20 cm until it is 10 years old. The females grow somewhat faster than the males.

Spawning is very noisy and takes place in shoals from the end of April to June. The eggs are generally laid in two or three batches. This intermittent spawning is a way of ensuring success-

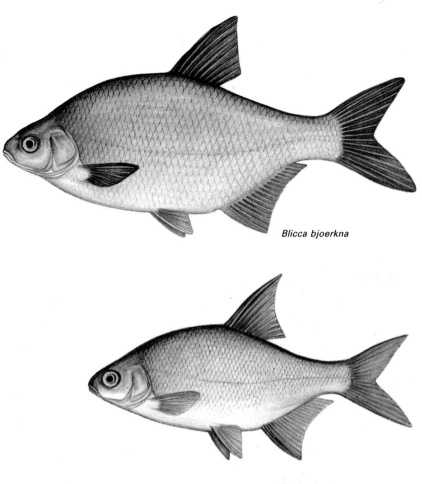

Blicca bjoerkna

B. bjoerkna juv.

ful development of the new generation in case the water level falls after the first spawning, for instance, and the eggs left sticking to exposed plants dry up and die. The development of the eggs, from spawning to hatching, takes 10—14 days, according to the temperature of the water. The Silver Bream occasionally interbreeds with other cyprinid fishes.

Although the Silver Bream is an abundant fish in many places, there are only a few regions where it is of any economic significance (e.g. the deltas of the Volga and the Dnepr). It is caught occasionally with rod and line, but anglers often use it as bait for catching predatory fishes.

Distribution of
V. vimba

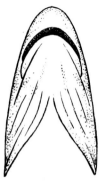

View of the underside
of the head of *V. vimba*

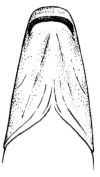

View of the underside
of the head of *C. nasus*

East European Bream; Zährte
Vimba vimba (L.)

○
Cyprinid fishes
Cyprinidae

The East European Bream has a distinctive, soft, ventral thick-lipped mouth below a prominent fleshy snout, an elongate body and a deeply forked, tapering caudal fin whose lower lobe is longer than the upper lobe. Its body is extremely flat-sided and behind its ventral fins there is a scaleless keel; on its back, in front of the dorsal fin, there is a striking scaleless groove. The colouring of the East European Bream changes markedly during the year. In the autumn, winter and spring it usually has a greyish blue back, silvery sides and a white belly, but at the beginning of the summer, in the spawning season, its back and sides turn so dark as to be almost black, while its throat, thorax and the under side of its tail are orange or ochre yellow and its originally yellowish or reddish paired fins turn a deep orange. The East European Bream usually grows to a length of about 30 cm and weighs up to 1 kg, but in rare cases can measure over 40 cm and weigh up to 3 kg.

In Europe the East European Bream occurs in the catchment areas of the Ems, Weser, Elbe and Vistula, the coun-

tries round the eastern part of the Baltic, the south of Sweden and Finland and Lake Ladoga. The subspecies *V. v. elongata* inhabits Alpine lakes in southern Bavaria and Upper Austria, *V. v. carinata* the Danube and other rivers emptying into the Black Sea as far as the Kuban and *V. v. melanops* the northern tributary rivers of the eastern part of the Mediterranean (the Vardar, Struma, Mesta and Maritza). Three more subspecies are distributed in the region of the Black Sea and the Caspian Sea.

The East European Bream is a relatively common fish in the quiet lower reaches of rivers, but it often moves upstream and is to be found below weirs. It lives in shoals near the bottom, in deep water over a hard, gravelly or stony bed. Its diet consists of various benthic invertebrates (mainly the larvae of aquatic insects, worms and small molluscs), occasionally supplemented by algae. It grows slowly and generally takes six years to reach a length of 20—25 cm.

The East European Bream spawns from April to June, and sometimes even until July, in flowing water with a hard,

110

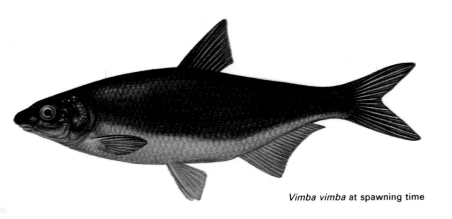

Vimba vimba at spawning time

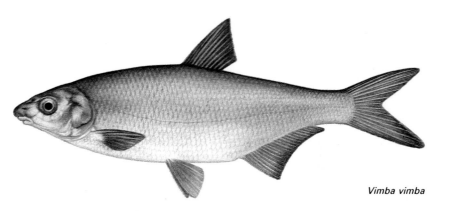

Vimba vimba

stony bed. The fish swim upstream in shoals, often for long distances, and the eggs are laid in batches on the stones. In the breeding season the males have a spawning rash. The fry hatch in a very short time—only two or three days after the eggs have been fertilized.

In central Europe the East European Bream is of only local importance and is netted while migrating. In the tributary rivers of the Black Sea, the Caspian Sea and the Sea of Azov, however, large quantities are caught every year.

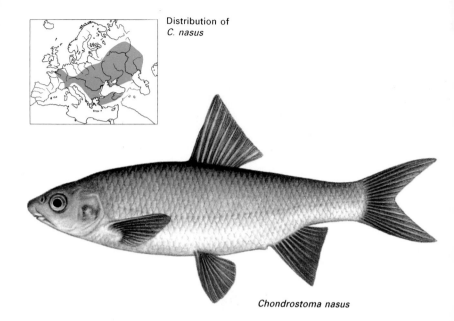

Chondrostoma nasus

Nase
Chondrostoma nasus (L.)

○ ■
Cyprinid fishes
Cyprinidae

The Nase, an abundant fish in submontane rivers in the basins of the Oder, the Vistula and the Danube, is less high-backed than the East European Bream and its sides are only slightly flattened. Its mouth, which is situated on the under side of its relatively small head, is narrow and hard, with horny lips. Its caudal fin is deeply forked. Its back is dark grey, with a bluish or greenish lustre, its sides are silvery and its belly is white or pale yellow; the dorsal and caudal fin are dark; the others are greyish red.

The Nase lives mostly in swiftly flowing water with a stony, sandy or slightly muddy bed, in the barbel and grayling zone, although it frequently invades the lower part of the trout zone. In the tributaries of the Oder, Vistula and Danube it is a very common fish in places.

Various subspecies have been described—*C. n. borysthenicus* in the Dnestr, Don and Danube delta, *C. n. ohridanum* in Lake Ohrid, *C. n. prespense* in Lake Prespa, *C. n. vardarense* in the river Vardar (and perhaps in the Struma, Mesta and Maritza as well) and *C. n. variabile* in the Volga, Ural and other rivers.

The Nase grows rather slowly, but has a long life span (up to 17 years). It can be up to 50 cm long and weigh over 2 kg, but usually measures 30—40 cm and weighs about 1 kg. It lives on algae, which it scrapes off from submerged stones together with the accompanying small fauna (caddis-worms, gnats, midges, etc.) with its horny lips, leaving characteristic 'grazing' marks behind it on the stones. If we watch a river while Nase are feeding, every now and again

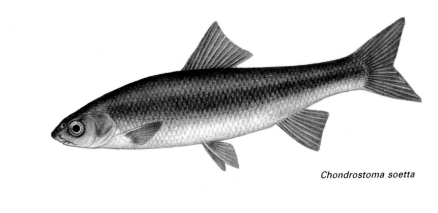

Chondrostoma soetta

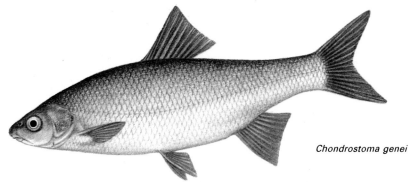

Chondrostoma genei

we can see a flash of white, as a grazing fish turns over for an instant on to its side.

Nase spawn at the age of four or five years, when they migrate upstream in masses from March to May. They spawn in turbulent, shallow water on a gravelly bed. While spawning they frequently leap out of the water. The brownish eggs are stuck to stones and the fry are hatched in 10—30 days, according to the temperature of the water. The young at first hide under stones.

South-western Europe, the eastern shores of the Black Sea and the western shores of the Caspian Sea are inhabited not by the Nase, but by a few related species—the Iberian peninsula by *C. polylepis* Steindachner, northwestern Spain and the west of France by *C. toxostoma* Vallot, Italy by *C. soetta* Bonaparte and *C. genei* Bonaparte, Dalmatia by *C. kneri* Heckel and *C. phoxinus* Heckel, the eastern shores of the Black Sea by *C. colchicum* (Kessler) and the basins of the rivers Kuma, Terek, Sulak and Rubas-chai along the western shore of the Caspian Sea by *C. oxyrhynchum* Kessler, which is not more than 25 cm long. The discrete ranges occupied by these related species is evidence that their geographical isolation must have taken place a comparatively long time ago.

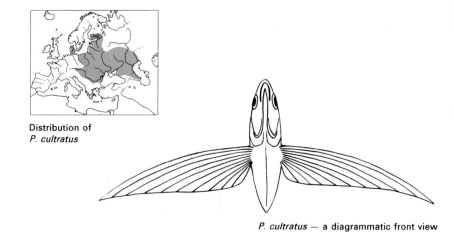

Distribution of
P. cultratus

P. cultratus — a diagrammatic front view

Ziege; Chekhon
Pelecus cultratus (L.)

● ○
Cyprinid fishes
Cyprinidae

Of all the cyprinid fishes of Europe, the Ziege is undoubtedly the most curious. It has a long, extremely flat-sided body, a completely straight back from its head onwards and a bulging belly. From its throat to its anal orifice runs a sharp, scaleless keel and it has a markedly superior mouth. Its short dorsal fin is set a long way back on its body, above the anal fin, but its most pronounced features are its sagging, zigzag lateral line and its very long pectoral fins. Its back is greyish silver or greyish green (sometimes greyish blue), its sides are silvery white and its belly is white. Its dorsal and caudal fins are greyish or greyish blue; its paired fins and anal fin are reddish. Its scales are very loose. The Ziege normally grows to a length of about 30 cm, but specimens about 11 years old, measuring 60 cm and weighing almost 2 kg, are also known.

The Ziege lives in brackish waters of the Baltic, the Black Sea, the Sea of Azov, the Caspian Sea and the Sea of Aral, but swims upstream to fresh water to spawn. It mostly frequents the surface layers of the water, but in the Sea of Azov it is known to undertake vertical migrations in association with the movements of the plankton; in the daytime it is to be found more in deep water and at night swims close to the surface.

The Ziege spawns at the age of three or four years, in parts of big rivers with a strong current. It is the only European freshwater fish with pelagic eggs, i.e. eggs which, after spawning and fertilization, float freely in the water, drifting with the current. When first expelled from the female's body, the eggs are only 1.3—1.5 mm in diameter, but in the water they immediately swell until they eventually measure over 5 mm across. The average number of eggs per female is considerable—about 30,000. The fry hatch in about one week.

At first, Ziege fry live on small planktonic organisms and young insect lar-

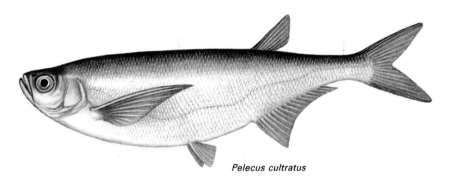

Pelecus cultratus

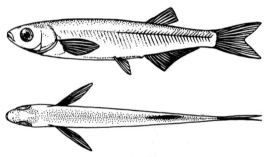

Top view of *P. cultratus* — juv.

vae. Later, when they measure about 13—14 cm, Ziege feed mainly on insects floating on the surface and often catch small fish. The Ziege is a tolerant fish as regards the oxygen content and quality of the water.

In central Europe it is not economically important, mainly because it is not very common. In the Danube and its tributaries it is likewise seldom netted in any great numbers. In south-eastern Europe, however, and especially in the lower reaches of rivers emptying into the Black Sea and the Sea of Azov, it is caught in large quantities, partly for human consumption (it tastes particularly good when smoked) and partly for its scales, which are used in the manufacture of artificial pearls, like those of the Bleak inhabiting Lake Ohrid. Ziege are caught with large seines, drop-nets, and gill nets, chiefly in the estuaries of large rivers.

Distribution of
A. aspius

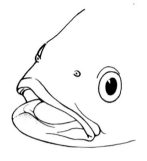

Front view of the head of *A. aspius*

Asp
Aspius aspius (L.)

○ ■
Cyprinid fishes
Cyprinidae

All the cyprinid fishes already described live either on small benthic fauna, plankton or aquatic plants, or—like the Chub, for instance—have a very varied diet. The adult Asp, however, lives mainly on fish and, like other predators, it has a slender, torpedo-shaped body. Furthermore, it grows to a remarkable size and in European waters we not infrequently come across specimens weighing 6—8 kg and measuring 60—80 cm; in exceptional cases the Asp may actually weigh about 15 kg and measure over 1 m.

The Asp has a large terminal mouth ending below its eyes. The lower jaw is a little longer than the upper jaw and has a thickened tip which fits into a depression in the upper jaw. The belly is rounded, but behind the ventral fins it has a scaly keel. The pectoral fins have pointed tips. The body is somewhat flat-sided and older fish are often rather high-backed. The Asp generally has a bluish or greyish blue back (in some waters greyish green), silvery sides and a white belly. The relatively high dorsal fin and the deeply forked caudal fin are greyish or greyish blue, with dark edges, and the other fins are reddish.

In Europe, the Asp's distribution area stretches eastwards from the basin of the Elbe as far as the Ural and northwards to the south of Norway, Sweden and Finland. It does not occur in western Europe (west of the Elbe and the Danube) or on any of the south European peninsulas.

The Asp mostly inhabits the lower reaches of big rivers, but is sometimes to be found in stagnant water, such as pools and old backwaters. Dams provide it with an ideal environment, especially for growth. It has a life span of about 15 years and grows relatively fast, with an annual weight increment of 0.5—1 kg. It reaches adulthood at 3—5 years. As a rule it remains near the surface of the water, catching small fish. It attacks its prey very noisily and frequently leaps out of the water; it also likes to gather large live and dead insects from the surface and big specimens will even catch frogs, mice and similar large animals.

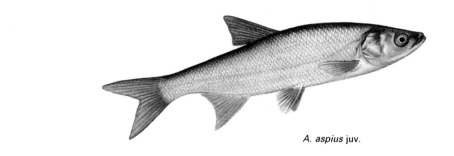

A. aspius juv.

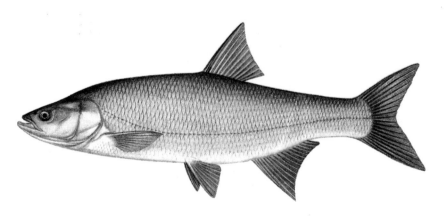

Aspius aspius

The Asp spawns from April to June in rivers with a strong current and a gravelly or stony bed. The eggs are stuck to stones or branches and similar objects. In the spawning season the males are peppered with spawning tubercles. The young feed initially on planktonic organisms and insect larvae and then on the fry of other fish; the adults are almost entirely piscivorous.

The commercial importance of the Asp increases in a west-to-east direction. A migratory form (*A. a. taeniatus*) inhabiting the southern part of the Caspian sea is commercially important in that region. It spawns in the rivers from March to April, is caught with various types of nets and is also popular with anglers.

Distribution of *T. tinca*

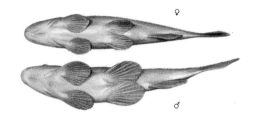
View of the underside of male and female *T. tinca.*

Tench
Tinca tinca (L.)

○ ■
Cyprinid fishes
Cyprinidae

The Tench is a sturdily built cyprinid fish with small scales firmly embedded in its skin and a relatively high, olive green body which is oval in cross section. The fins all have rounded edges and are slate grey to reddish violet. One short barbel is present at either corner of the mouth. The eyes are round and relatively small. The Tench has a dark, greyish green back, olive green, green or yellow-green sides with a golden sheen and a creamy white or yellow belly. Specimens living in deep ponds and in densely overgrown pools are often very dark, with fins so dark as to be almost black, whereas fish from shallow water with little vegetation are a very light greenish yellow colour and their lips and the surrounding area are yellowish red. Colour variants of the Tench (gold, red, or orange with dark spots on back and sides) are occasionally kept in fishponds and ornamental ponds. Scaleless Tench and Tench with a reduced number of scales, as known in the various races of the Domesticated Carp, have also been described and a veil-tailed form is likewise known.

The Tench is distributed over the whole of Europe with the exception of the north of Scotland, the northern parts of Scandinavia, the Dalmatian coast of Yugoslavia and the southern part of the Balkan peninsula and the Crimea. In central Europe it grows to an average length of 30—40 cm and weighs 1—2 kg (occasionally more), but the one that measured 70 cm and weighed over 7 kg was an exceptional catch.

The Tench is one of the few European fishes which display distinct sexual dimorphism outside the breeding season. In the male, the second, unbranched rays of the ventral fins are noticeably thicker than in the female and the ventral fins themselves are altogether larger; if we fold them along the body, they extend beyond the anus in the male, but do not even reach it in the female.

The Tench is to be encountered in virtually every type of European water, including the trout zone, but it shows a preference for warm and quiet water. Given good conditions, it grows fairly quickly and reaches market size (300 g) by its third year. It also tolerates dense vegetation and a very poor oxygen supply, i.e. an environment in which the Carp could not exist. Its diet consists chiefly of bottom-dwelling organisms.

Tinca tinca

Tinca tinca — a golden form

Spawning takes place from the end of May to July, in shallow, overgrown water warmed by the sun, at the edge of ponds, rivers and pools. The female deposits large numbers of tiny eggs about 1 mm in diameter on water weeds. The fry, which hatch 4—8 days after the eggs have been fertilized, remain clinging to the aquatic vegetation and do not swim away for about 14—17 days.

The economic significance of the Tench is considerable; it is often kept as an additional fish in carp ponds and in some countries (Germany, France) it is consumed on a large scale. It is also popular with anglers who catch it mostly on the bottom with animal baits.

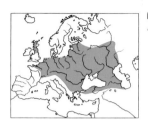

Bitterling
Rhodeus sericeus amarus (BLOCH)

Cyprinid fishes
Cyprinidae

The Bitterling is a small fish usually measuring only 5—6 cm (rarely up to 8 cm); with its high-backed, deep-bellied body it looks rather like a miniature Bream. It has a small, semi-ventral mouth and relatively large eyes and its body is covered with large scales. Its dorsal and anal fin are similarly shaped, although the dorsal fin is somewhat longer and higher. Its lateral line is incomplete and is usually distinguishable only on the first five or six scales.

The Bitterling has a greyish green to dark greenish grey back, fading to greyish silver on the sides, and a white belly, often with a touch of pink. Its scales have a dark grey border, so that they form a reticular pattern on the body and give the sides a greyish tinge. On either side of the rear half of the body there is a bluish green band shaped like a narrow isosceles triangle, with the apex pointing forward and the base in the middle of the root of the tail, at the point of attachment of the caudal fin. The dorsal and anal fin are grey; the caudal fin and the paired fins are reddish or faintly orange. In the spawning season, Bitterlings are particularly gaudily coloured and are showier than most other European freshwater fishes. Their throat, chest and belly turn bright red, the whole of their back is a gleaming opalescent bluish green to violet and the colour of the band on their sides deepens. The females remain plainly coloured, but develop a long ovipositor.

The Bitterling frequents still water, in the lower reaches of rivers, creeks with a muddy bed, old backwaters, pools and weedy lakes inhabited by Swan Mussels and freshwater Pearl Mussels, without which it would be unable to reproduce. The interesting reproduction of the Bitterling has been described in detail in the chapter dealing with the way in which fish care for their offspring (p. 15). The Bitterling's spawning season lasts from April to June and the eggs are laid singly in the mussels' branchial cavity, where they are fertilized and develop; the fry remain inside the shell until they are able to fend for themselves. Bitterlings live on small planktonic organisms (mainly phytoplankton).

In Europe, the Bitterling's range stretches eastwards from the valley of the Rhône. It is abundant in the region of the Black Sea and the Caspian Sea and is also found in the eastern part of the Balkan peninsula, east of the basin of the river Vardar. It does not occur south of the Alps and the Pyrenees, in Denmark or in Scandinavia, but it has been introduced into the British Isles.

The Bitterling is a popular fish in cold-water aquaria and is also kept in school aquaria, chiefly because of its interesting reproduction biology. Anglers seldom employ it as bait, because they know that predators do not like its bitter-tasting flesh.

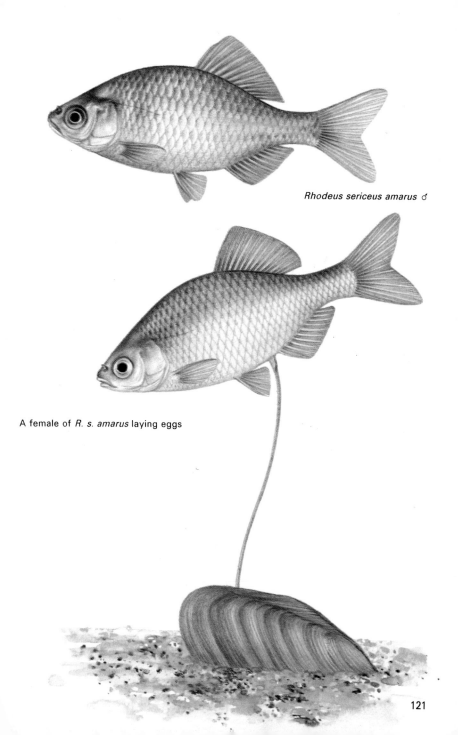

Rhodeus sericeus amarus ♂

A female of *R. s. amarus* laying eggs

121

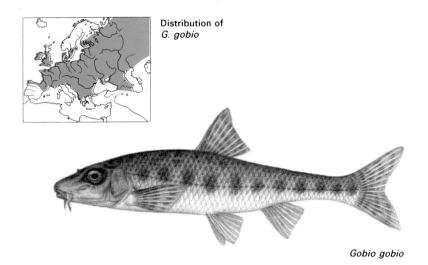

Distribution of
G. gobio

Gobio gobio

Gudgeon
Gobio gobio (L.)

►
Cyprinid fishes
Cyprinidae

Gudgeon are small cyprinid fishes with a long fusiform body, relatively large scales and a short dorsal and anal fin. They have a single barbel at either corner of their mouth and their pharyngeal teeth are arranged in two rows. Of their five European representatives, the commonest and most widespread is the Gudgeon, which inhabits practically the whole of Europe except the Iberian peninsula, Italy, Greece, the north of Scotland, Norway and the north of Sweden and Finland. It lives in stagnant water and in rivers and streams from the bream zone to the lower part of the trout zone.

As distinct from related species, the Gudgeon has a comparatively high-backed and slightly flat-sided body. In keeping with its benthic habits, its belly is straight. On either side of its inferior mouth there is a single short barbel, which stretches no further than its eye. Its throat is scaleless, except for the middle, where we can sometimes find scales. Its back is brown or greyish

brown and sometimes greenish; its silvery or yellowish sides are adorned with a long row of six to twelve large dark spots. The fins are greyish yellow or faintly pinkish. The small spots on the caudal fin are arranged in several rows running parallel to the notch in the fin.

At the age of two or three years the Gudgeon spawns in May or June in shallow water with a stony bed. The eggs are attached to stones and the roots of plants; the fry live in shoals near the bottom, in shallow water. They at first subsist on planktonic organisms and small insect larvae, but later feed mainly on bottom-dwelling organisms, such as midge, caddis-fly and mayfly larvae. With a life span of not more than five years, the Gudgeon is a short-lived fish. Its maximum length is 20 cm, but it usually does not measure more than 10—12 cm. It has high oxygen requirements, but can tolerate polluted water quite well. It is very popular as bait for catching predatory fishes.

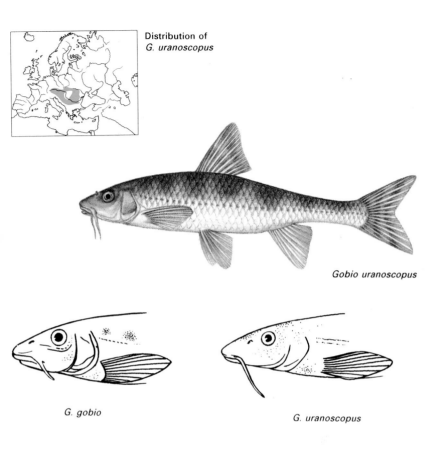

Gobio uranoscopus

G. gobio

G. uranoscopus

Danube Longbarbel Gudgeon
Gobio uranoscopus (AGASSIZ)

Cyprinid fishes
Cyprinidae

The Danube Gudgeon, which inhabits the Danube basin, prefers submontane rivers with a fast current, where it lives near the bed. It has a scaly throat and very long barbels stretching to the posterior edge of the anterior opercular bone, a long way behind the eye. It has a slender body and a long, narrow head; its eyes lie close together and face upwards. The spots at the hind end of its body often merge to form two parallel longitudinal stripes. The fins are dingy yellow and on the dorsal and caudal fin there are two brownish cross stripes. This gudgeon grows to a length of 12—15 cm.

The subspecies *G. u. frici* inhabits Czechoslovakia, the Transcarpathian Ukraine, Romania and Bulgaria; the nominate subspecies lives in the upper Danube basin. This species does not form large shoals like the Gudgeon. Its diet consists of benthic animals, but otherwise little is known of its biology.

Distribution of
G. kessleri

Distribution of
G. albipinnatus

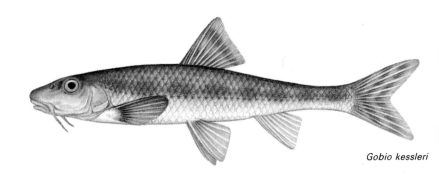

Gobio kessleri

Kessler's Gudgeon
Gobio kessleri DYBOWSKI

Cyprinid fishes
Cyprinidae

Kessler's Gudgeon resembles the two preceding species, but can be distinguished from them by its bare throat and the length of its barbels, which are longer than those of the Gudgeon, but shorter than those of the Danube Longbarbel Gudgeon (they reach only a little way beyond the posterior edge of the eye). This fish has a greyish black, indistinctly dark-spotted back, greyish silver sides and a white belly. On its dorsal and caudal fins there are one to three dark stripes composed of dark brown or black spots. Kessler's Gudgeon grows to a length of 13—15 cm.

It inhabits the catchment areas of the Vistula, Danube and Dnestr and occurs in swiftly flowing rivers rich in oxygen, where it forms shoals near the bed; it lives on creatures occurring at the bottom. *Gobio kessleri antipai* is known from the delta of the Danube and *G. kessleri banaticus* from some of its tributaries.

C. ciscaucasicus Berg, an inhabitant of the basins of the rivers Kuban, Kuma and Terek, etc, in the USSR, measures about 15 cm and has long barbels and a strikingly long, thin root to its tail. It likewise forms shoals and lives on bottom-dwelling animals.

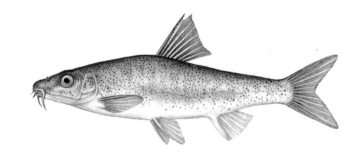

Aulopyge hügeli

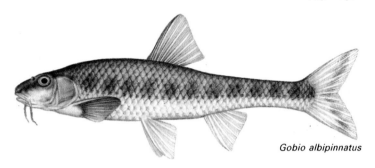

Gobio albipinnatus

Whitefin Gudgeon
Gobio albipinnatus LUKASCH

Cyprinid fishes
Cyprinidae

The Whitefin Gudgeon, which at first glance looks like all the other gudgeons, has a scaleless throat and a flat-sided tail; the spots on its sides taper away posteriorly. Its barbels stretch to the far edge of its eyes and its lateral line is bordered by small dark spots; similar spots form a dark band parallel to the notch in its caudal fin. Its biology is the same as that of other gudgeons, but it prefers deeper water and is consequently to be found mainly in the middle and lower reaches of the rivers.

The Whitefin Gudgeon is distributed in the basins of the Volga, Dnepr and Don and in the Danube from Czechoslovakia as far as the mouth. The lower reaches of Danube tributaries are inhabited by the subspecies *G. a. vladykovi* and another subspecies occurs in

the basins of the Bug and the Dnepr in the USSR.

The Dalmatian Barbelgudgeon, *Aulopyge hügeli* Heckel is a small fish related to the gudgeons, which lives at the bottom of flowing water in the Yugoslavian provinces of Bosnia and Dalmatia. It is somewhat flat-sided and the longest ray in its dorsal fin is toothed. It has an inferior mouth with four short barbels. The females of this species are very different in appearance from the males; they have a higher back and a striking cloacal process on their anal fin. *A. hügeli* measures 10—13 cm. Its silvery body is marked with irregular brownish black spots; its back is darker and greenish and there is a dark, wide, oval stripe on its sides. Dark spots are present on the unpaired fins.

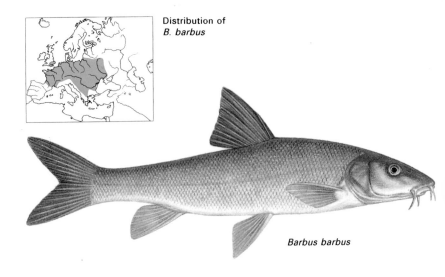

Distribution of
B. barbus

Barbus barbus

Barbel
Barbus barbus (L.)

○ ■
Cyprinid fishes
Cyprinidae

The Barbel has a noticeably long, low, cylindrical body and head and a markedly ventral protrusible mouth with four barbels. Its eyes are situated high up on its head and face slightly upwards, indicating—like the shape of the body—that the Barbel is a fish living at the bottom. The caudal fin is deeply forked; the last hard ray of the dorsal fin is thick, with a clearly toothed posterior edge. The barbel has an olive green to dark greyish blue back, lighter sides and a white belly. The sides of adult specimens have a golden lustre, young fish have dark spots and are sometimes mottled. The dorsal and caudal fin are grey, with dark edges; the other fins are reddish. The Barbel grows to over 80 cm and can weigh over 4 kg (in exceptional cases more).

The area of the nominate subspecies extends eastwards from France and south-eastern England to the river Neman (Memel) in Lithuania (USSR) and the Danube basin; *B. b. bocagei* and *B.*

b. sclateri inhabit Spain and Portugal, *B. b. macedonicus* the basin of the river Vardar in the Balkans and two more subspecies—*B. b. bergi* and *B. b. borysthenicus*—the Black Sea region.

The Barbel lives on the bed of swiftly flowing rivers at low altitudes (the barbel zone) and from here swims upstream to the grayling zone and sometimes to the lower parts of the trout zone. It lives mainly on various bottom-dwelling creatures; large specimens also catch crayfish, molluscs and small fish. The Barbel becomes sexually mature at the age of 4—7 years. The fish migrate up-river and spawning takes place from May to August in fairly shallow water with a sandy and stony bed. The males can be distinguished by the whitish spawning rash on their head and back. The eggs are stuck to stones and sand on the bottom and the fry are usually hatched in six to eight days. In some places this is an important species for both fishermen and anglers.

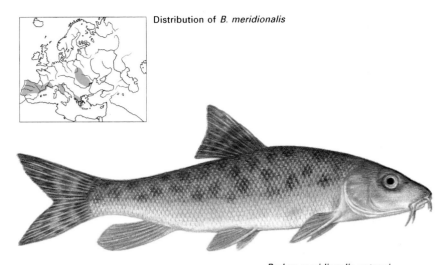

Barbus meridionalis petenyi

Dorsal fin of *B. barbus*

Dorsal fin of *B. meridionalis petenyi*

Southern Barbel
Barbus meridionalis Risso

Cyprinid fishes
Cyprinidae

The Southern Barbel, which measures about 30 cm (seldom 40 cm), is the most widespread of the smaller European barbels. Its colouring is different from that of the Barbel and the last hard ray in its dorsal fin is not toothed. Its anal fin is very long and if folded against the body it stretches to the base of the caudal fin. The Southern Barbel occurs in Spain, Portugal, the south of France, northern Italy and the basins of the Danube, Dnestr, Vistula, Vardar and the rivers of southern Bulgaria, Albania and Greece. The subspecies *B. m. petenyi*, illustrated here, inhabits the catchment areas of the Vistula, Dnestr and Danube. It frequents the river bed in small shoals and lives on benthos.

Further small barbel species are distributed here and there in southern Europe and in the region round the Caspian Sea.

127

Distribution of *C. carpio* (Wild Carp)

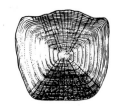

A cycloid scale

Wild Carp
Cyprinus carpio L.

◐ ○ ■
Cyprinid fishes
Cyprinidae

The Carp is the economically most important freshwater fish in Europe. The original wild form, from the region round the Black Sea, the Sea of Azov, the Caspian Sea and the Aral Sea, has an elongate, fusiform body, which is almost circular in cross section and is always covered with scales throughout. Four fleshy barbels are appended to the mouth. The dorsal fin is very long and the cycloid scales covering the body are relatively large and firmly embedded in the skin. The lateral line runs the entire length of the sides. The wild Carp has a dark (sometimes very dark) greenish brown or greyish green back, lighter, more dingy olive sides with a golden sheen and a yellowish white or creamy white belly. The unpaired fins are greyish blue, the paired fins reddish; the anal and caudal fin are sometimes also reddish. The wild Carp is a robust fish measuring up to a whole metre or more and weighing 20 kg (in rare cases over 30 kg). In its first year it grows very quickly, but in subsequent years its weight increments are smaller than those of domesticated Carp.

The Carp is sexually mature by its third or fourth year—the males usually a year sooner than the females. It spawns in May and in June, in shallow littoral water with plenty of vegetation, at water temperatures of about 15 °C. Spawning is a very noisy affair and during it the fish often leap high into the air. The eggs are attached to water weeds and at a water temperature of 15 °C the fry are hatched in five days (at 20 °C in three). On hatching they measure about 5 mm and have a large yolk sac and special glands enabling them to cling to the plants. They remain attached for between three and fourteen days, according to the water temperature whilst the yolk is absorbed. When the yolk sac has been digested, they swim away and begin to take in microscopic food—first of all the smallest and then larger zooplankton; by the time they measure about 2 cm they begin to devour bottom-dwelling animals. Food intake is closely associated with the temperature of the water; in the autumn Carp stop eating, retire to deeper places and become inactive.

Carp inhabit deep slow-flowing and stagnant water; they live in the course of the river and in its accompanying backwaters, side arms and pools. They frequent the deeper parts and remain close to the bed, where they look for

Cyprinus carpio — a wild form

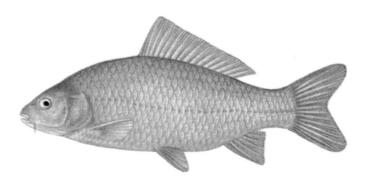

C. carpio — an artificially bred golden form

food in the mud; their diet consists largely of aquatic insect larvae, aquatic molluscs, crustaceans and worms etc, although plants are also an important component. Wild carp go in search of food mainly in the evening and at night.

The wild form of the Carp is of real economic significance only in south-eastern Europe, where it is caught with nets and with rod and line. It is popular with anglers partly because it is a very shy and wary fish and consequently hard to catch, and partly because it is powerfully built and puts up a good fight.

An artificially bred golden form is occasionally kept in gardens and parks.

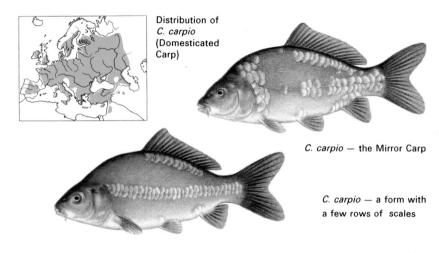

Distribution of
C. carpio
(Domesticated
Carp)

C. carpio — the Mirror Carp

C. carpio — a form with
a few rows of scales

Domesticated Carp
Cyprinus carpio L.

○ ■
Cyprinid fishes
Cyprinidae

The majority of European pond-bred Carp races probably came from the Danube, where the Romans caught carp and introduced them to ponds over practically the whole of the continent. Centuries of selective breeding have produced the present-day quickly growing, deep-bellied and high-backed Carp which are the most important freshwater fish to be kept in ponds. Modern man has continued the Roman's introductions to suitable open waters all over Europe. The cradle of modern European pond fish-breeding was undoubtedly Bohemia (now part of Czechoslovakia), where it already existed in the twelfth century. Under the Emperor Charles IV, who encouraged the foundation of big fishpond systems in central and eastern Bohemia in the fourteenth century, it became a flourishing industry joined, in the sixteenth century, by the now world-famous ponds of southern Bohemia.

In addition to the more widespread scaly races of domesticated Carp, we may come across various scale aberrations. There are scaleless Carp, on whose body we should look in vain for a single scale, Carp with just one row of large scales along their sides and another row of smaller scales below their dorsal fin, and Leather Carp, which have only isolated large scales below their dorsal fin and along the base of their other fins. Between these types there are a whole series of intermediate forms, such as Mirror Carp, for instance. All pond-bred carp differ from the original wild form in two basic respects, however—their relatively short, high, wide body and their growth rate, which is high not only in the first year, but in every subsequent year as well.

According to their function and the age of their occupants, carp ponds are divided into spawning ponds (used for spawning of the mother fish), fry ponds (in which the young are kept for their first year), deep overwintering ponds (in which stock is kept during the winter) and main ponds (in which fish ready for marketing, weighing 1—2.5 kg, are kept).

The basic requirement for high fish production in fishponds is an adequate

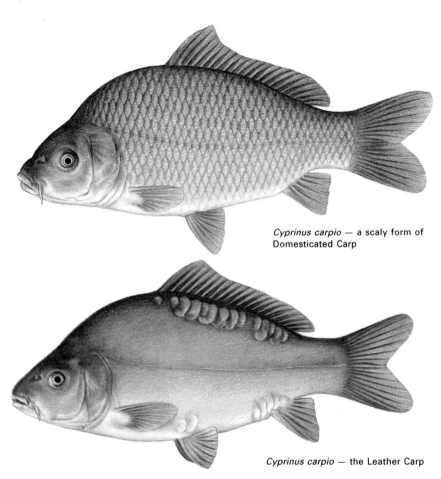

Cyprinus carpio — a scaly form of Domesticated Carp

Cyprinus carpio — the Leather Carp

supply of natural food, i.e. planktonic and bottom-dwelling animals. It is, therefore, essential to ensure the best possible conditions for development of the primary link in the pond's food chain, i.e. phytoplankton, since this is the food of the small planktonic and benthic animals on which the fish live. Carp breeders therefore fertilize, lime and add supplementary nutrients to the water and improve its quality in general. One of the most effective ways of assuring a good increase in pond fish production is to give the fish extra food. Nowadays this is provided almost solely in the form of granulated foods containing all the important components needed by the fish, including medicinal substances, vitamins and trace elements. Another way to increase production is to introduce suitable quick-growing secondary fish into the pond, alongside the Carp. Predators (Pike, Pikeperch, Catfish and Rainbow Trout) help control numbers of small, and hence slow-growing Carp, while in ponds with an excess of water weeds or phytoplankton, herbivorous species like the Grass Carp and Silver Carp are a help.

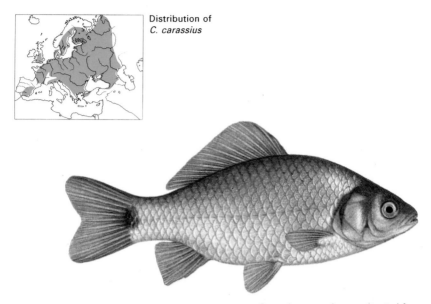

Distribution of
C. carassius

Carassius carassius — a stunted form

Crucian Carp
Carassius carassius (L.)

○ ▶
Cyprinid fishes
Cyprinidae

The Crucian Carp is immediately distinguishable from the Carp by the absence of barbels. It is a different colour from the related Goldfish, but that alone is not enough to separate the two species. A more reliable criterion is the shape of the dorsal fin, which is convex in the Crucian Carp and has a slight concavity in the Goldfish. Furthermore, the last hard ray in the dorsal fin of the Crucian Carp has about 30 teeth of equal size on its posterior edge—in the Goldfish only 10—15, increasing in size from the bottom upwards.

The Crucian Carp usually has a brownish black back, golden or greyish green sides and a yellowish or white belly.

It inhabits stagnant and slow-flowing water over practically the whole of Europe from Scandinavia to the Alps, and stretches eastwards into Asia as far as the basin of the river Lena. It is, however, absent from the more northerly parts of Scandinavia, the north of Scotland, Ireland, the western part of the Iberian peninsula, central and southern Italy and the western and southern part of the Balkan peninsula.

In ponds, sluggish rivers and backwaters, the Crucian Carp usually grows to a length of about 40 cm and weighs about 1 kg. In such waters, where it has a good food supply, it is robust, with a short, high-backed body. However, it can also tolerate unfavourable condi-

132

Carassius carassius

tions in shallow water overgrown with vegetation, where for most of the year the water is oxygen deficient and contains high levels of carbon dioxide and hydrogen sulphide. In such water we find a stunted form of the Crucian Carp (*Carassius c.* m. *humilis* Heckel), whose body is a very different shape from that of the pond-bred Crucian Carp; it has a relatively slim, long body and grows very slowly, so that at the age of eight to ten years it measures only 9—10 cm. The dwarf Crucian Carp can also survive short periods frozen in ice.

The Crucian Carp is a bottom-dwelling fish and lives mainly on benthic fauna, although water plants also form a relatively large part of its diet. Dwarf Crucian Carp live chiefly on small zooplankton. Spawning takes place in May and June. Crucian Carp are phytophilous fish, i.e. they attach their eggs, which are laid in several consecutive batches, to submerged plants. The fry are hatched in 5—7 days.

The Crucian Carp used to be kept in carp ponds together with the Carp and the two actually interbreed. The species is sometimes used by anglers for catching predators. In western and central Europe its commercial significance is small, but in eastern Europe it is an economically important fish and is fished with nets. It is a suitable fish for introduction to water with a poor oxygen supply.

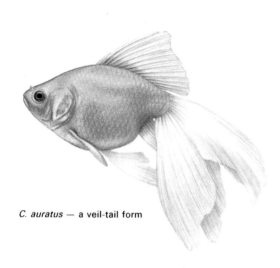

C. auratus — a veil-tail form

Distribution of
C. auratus

Goldfish
Carassius auratus (L.)

Cyprinid fishes
Cyprinidae

Whereas the sides of the Crucian Carp are predominantly golden, those of the ancestral Goldfish are greyish silver. In the more familiar aquarium variety, the whole body is a brilliant orange. The Goldfish also has a more cylindrical and less flat-sided body than the Crucian Carp; it grows faster and attains sexual maturity in its third or fourth year. Originally an inhabitant of eastern Asia, it has been introduced to eastern, northern and central Europe and is still advancing westwards.

Like the Crucian Carp, Goldfish spawn intermittently in May and June and attach the eggs to aquatic plants. It likewise lives on the same food as the Crucian Carp. Contrary to the data in the earlier literature, it also occurs in large quantities in small and muddy pools, as well as in big rivers and open

lakes. Because of the difficulty of telling it apart from the Crucian Carp, however, knowledge of its distribution in Europe is still inexact.

In the Danube basin there are probably three distribution centres of naturalised Goldfish. In the 1950's it occurred only in the delta and from there spread gradually up the Danube, against the current. The second centre is the Hungarian fishpond region on the river Körös, from which Goldfish invaded the river Tisa and its tributaries, travelling upstream to Slovakia and downstream to the middle reaches of the Danube and some of its tributaries in Yugoslavia. The third probable centre of distribution of naturalised Goldfish in the catchment area of the Danube are a number of Bulgarian fishpond systems, from which the fish spread to

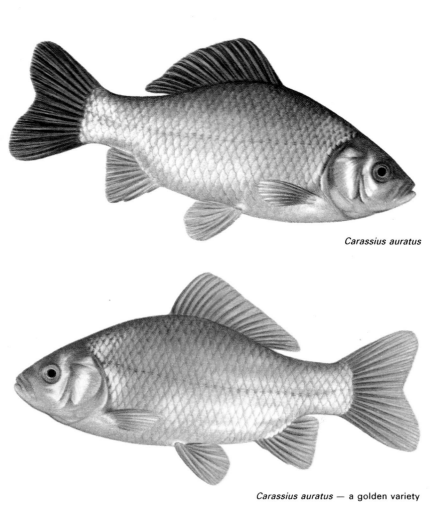

Carassius auratus

Carassius auratus — a golden variety

a great many Bulgarian rivers and a long segment of the Danube. The only place where naturalised Goldfish are of any economic significance is the south-eastern part of Europe. The golden variety of the Goldfish, which is particularly popular with aquarists and is also kept in gardens and parks, was first bred over 600 years ago. Particularly popular are the various types of veil-tails as well as fish with telescopic eyes, and fish with colour and size variations.

Distribution of
N. barbatulus

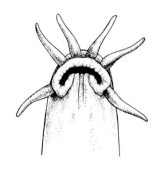

View of the underside of the head of
N. barbatulus

Stone Loach
Noemacheilus barbatulus (L.)

The Stone Loach, the Commonest European loach, is a mottled little fish measuring 12—18 cm and occasionally more, inhabiting both stagnant and flowing water. It has an elongate body with a flattened belly and brownish yellow sides marked with characteristic blackish brown marbling; its back is generally brownish or brownish green and there are rows of small dark spots on its dorsal and caudal fin, which is straight-ended. Its belly is usually greyish white, but is sometimes tinged with pink. The suborbital spines, pronounced in related loaches, are reduced in the Stone Loach.

In Europe, the Stone Loach's distribution extends eastwards from Great Britain and north-eastern Spain to the river Ural and from there into Asia; it does not occur in the north of Scotland, in Norway, the more northern parts of Sweden and Finland, central and southern Italy and the south of Greece. It remains near the bottom and spends most of its time hidden under stones and overhanging banks, or among

roots. Its environmental requirements are very modest and it even tolerates relatively highly polluted water. It is to be found in lowland rivers and high up in the mountains in the trout zone. Its diet consists mainly of the larvae of aquatic insects and worms (e.g. threadworms). It spawns from March to May on a sandy or stony bed; the eggs are stuck to grit and small stones and are guarded by the male. Spawning takes place intermittently and the eggs are laid in several consecutive batches.

The Stone Loach forms several subspecies over its large range. *N. b. sturanyi* lives in Lake Ohrid, *N. b. vardarensis* in the basin of the river Vardar and *N. b. caucasicus* in the tributaries of the river Terek in the Caucasus.

Two further members of the same genus extend into European territory. The Angora Loach, *N. angorae*, is distributed in Asia Minor and the Black Sea region, while its only subspecies, *N. a. bureschi*, regarded by some zoologists as a separate species, lives in the basin of the river Struma in Bulgaria. This relatively

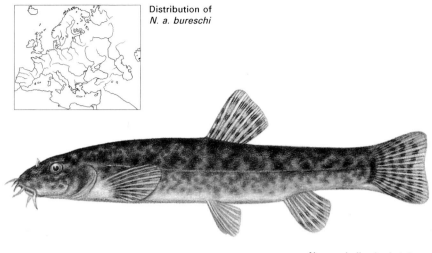

Distribution of
N. a. bureschi

Noemacheilus barbatulus

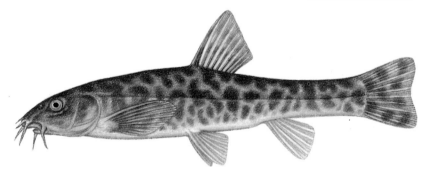

Noemacheilus angorae bureschi

short and thickset, rather light-coloured little fish measuring 7—8.5 cm has a yellowish body marked with a few rows of irregularly distributed dark spots, the largest of which lie along the lateral line. It inhabits shallow water with a strong current in parts of the river Struma and its small tributaries.

The last European member of this genus, the Terek Loach *N. merga* (Krynicki), which occurs in the northern Caucasus in the basins of the rivers Ku-

ban, Kuma, Terek and Sulak, is a kind of intermediate form between the Stone Loach and the Angora Loach. So far practically nothing is known of its biology.

These little fish are all important as food for bigger fish; the Stone Loach, for instance, is an important item on the menu of the Brown Trout. In some places anglers use stone loaches as bait for catching predators.

Distribution of
M. fossilis

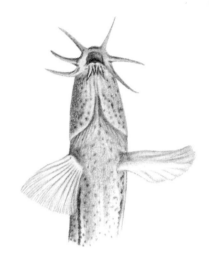

View of the underside of the body of
M. fossilis

Weatherfish
Misgurnus fossilis (L.)

With a length of 20—25 cm (exceptionally over 30 cm), the Weatherfish is the biggest member of the loach family. It has a long, cylindrical body with posteriorly slightly flattened sides. Like male Stone Loaches, the males have somewhat longer pectoral fins than the females. The Weatherfish has a brownish (sometimes almost black, sometimes brownish red) head with a ventral mouth surrounded by ten barbels—four on the upper jaw, two at the corners of the mouth and four short ones on the lower lip. The back is generally brown or brownish black, while the sides and belly are yellow or orange-red. A broad dark brown to black band, bordered on either side by a thin dark stripe, stretches along the sides from the eyes to the base of the caudal fin. The light-coloured belly is covered with small

dark spots; the yellowish brown fins are also marked with dark spots.

In Europe, the Weatherfish is distributed from north-eastern France as far as the river Neva in the USSR; it also lives in the basins of the Danube, the Don and the Volga. It is absent from Scandinavia, the British Isles, western France and the Iberian peninsula, Italy, the southern parts of the Balkans and the Crimea.

Weatherfish are at home in muddy water, such as the lower reaches of rivers, old backwaters, irrigation canals, ponds, pools, the connecting canals between fishponds and similar habitats. Before sudden and severe changes in atmospheric pressure they surface, and if their oxygen supply is poor they audibly gulp air and absorb the necessary oxygen from their intestine. The

138

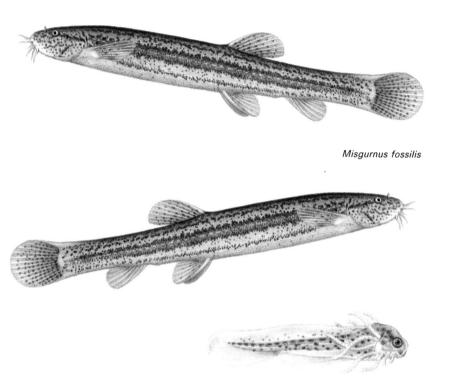

Misgurnus fossilis

An embryo of *M. fossilis*

Weatherfish is a nocturnal fish; during the daytime it goes into hiding on the bottom or in some other kind of shelter. It lives on various invertebrates, including insect larvae, molluscs, worms, etc. If we pick up a live Weatherfish, it emits a characteristic whistling sound made by the air as it is expelled.

Weatherfish spawn in May and June, when they often collect in large numbers in shallows and flooded meadows. The females each lay 5,000 to 30,000 eggs, according to their size, and stick them to the vegetation. The newly hatched young fish has a very bizarre appearance; on its head we can see special filamentous external gills, auxilliary organs of respiration which disappear within a few days, when the fry disperse and begin to feed on small bottom-dwelling organisms.

The Weatherfish is distributed over a very large area, but its population is homogeneous and no subspecies have been described. Throughout its range it is not common and is not caught on a large scale. In places where it is abundant, anglers like to use it as live bait for catching predators; a Weatherfish wriggling tenaciously on the end of a hook represents an enticing morsel for a pike.

Distribution of
C. taenia

A detail of the head of *C. taenia*

Spined Loach
Cobitis taenia L.

Loaches
Cobitidae

The members of the genus from which the whole loach family (Cobitidae) takes its name have a small, elongate, markedly flat-sided body and head and six barbels round their mouth. Below each eye lies a well developed erectile bony spine with a forked tip, whose defensive purpose is soon made clear if the fish is handled. In its efforts to escape, the loach inflicts painful pricks with the short, but sharp spines.

The Spined Loach is distributed over almost the whole of Europe and also occurs in Asia; the only places where it does not occur are Ireland, the north of Scotland, Norway, northern Sweden, Finland and the north of the European part of the USSR. It forms several geographical races within its range. The subspecies *C. t. bilineata* is known from northern Italy, *C. t. dalmatina* from the river Cetina in Dalmatia, *C. t. haasi* from the east of Spain, *C. t. meridionalis* from Lake Prespa, *C. t. paludicola* from the basin of the river Tajo in Spain, *C. t. puta* from the basin of the Po in northern Italy and *C. t. strumicae* from the basin of the river Struma in Bulgaria.

The Spined Loach has a brownish grey, dark-mottled back and sometimes has dark cross stripes on its sides.

Along its sides run two rows (sometimes only one row) of 10—20 large, round dark spots and a striking black spot can be seen at the point of attachment of the caudal fin; its belly is white or yellowish. Like other members of the genus, the Spined Loach only has a vestigial swim-bladder and if it wishes to surface, it has to do so by wriggling.

The Spined Loach grows to a length of about 10 cm. It lives in stagnant and sluggish water with a sandy or stony bed (less often with a muddy bed). Very often it buries itself completely in the sand, leaving only the front of its head and its eyes showing. Its food consists of small bottom-dwelling animals—insect larvae, small worms and molluscs. It spawns in May and June.

Several closely related species live in southern and south-eastern Europe. The largest of these, the Balkan Loach *C. elongata* Heckel et Kner, from the Danube basin in Yugoslavia, north-western Romania and northern Bulgaria, measures almost 17 cm. The Romanian Loach *C. romanica* Bacescu, which measures about 12 cm and has relatively very short barbels, inhabits Romanian tributaries of the Danube.

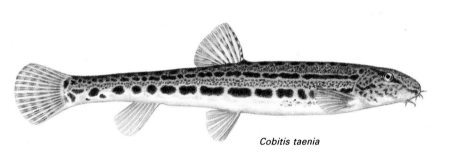

Cobitis taenia

Cobitis elongata

Cobitis romanica

From northern Italy comes the Italian Loach *C. larvata* Filippi, which is maximally 8 cm long and is brownish red, with 8—10 irregular dark spots along its sides. Further small species of the same genus inhabit the regions round the Black Sea and the Caspian Sea.

These small fishes are not economically important, but they are sometimes successfully kept in aquaria.

Distribution of
S. aurata

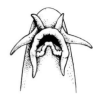

View of the underside of the head of
S. aurata

East European Spined Loach; Golden Loach
Sabanejewia (*Cobitis*) *aurata* (Filippi)

Loaches
Cobitidae

The East European Spined Loach is easily distinguished from the Spined Loach by its colouring; the latter has small, elongate spots along its sides, while in the former the spots are fewer in number, larger and squarer. On the inner surface of the second ray of its pectoral fins, the Spined Loach has a curious rounded disc, known as a Canestrini scale, which is absent in its cousin.

The ground colour of the East European Spined Loach is greyish white. Its sides and belly are tinged with yellow, while its back is grey, with 4—12 dark brown spots. Its barbels are longer than those of the Spined Loach. On the under side of the root of its tail there is a thin adipose keel.

The nominate form of this loach lives in Caucasian rivers and the basin of the Don. *S. a. bulgarica* occurs in the middle and lower reaches of the Danube, *S. a. balcanica* lives in the tributaries of the Danube from Czechoslovakia all the way to the delta, in the Vardar, Struma, Mesta and Maritza and probably in the Vistula and Neman (Memel) as well,

while two more subspecies—*S. a. radnensis* and *S. a. vallachia*—have been described in Romania. The systematic position of these subspecies is at present somewhat uncertain and research studies have shown that the taxonomy of the genera *Cobitis* and *Sabanejewia* is still fraught with controversial questions and problems.

The East European Spined Loach lives both in deep flowing water and in shallows, among stones and pebbles; it is mostly to be found in the barbel and the grayling zone, but sometimes in the lower reaches also. It likes to hide under stones and feeds mainly on small bottom-dwelling animals.

S. caspia Eichwald, which occurs in the Caspian Sea and its western and northern tributary rivers, measures only about 6.5 cm. It has dark stripes on its sides and a large black spot on the root of its tail, near the base of the caudal fin. The somewhat larger *S. caucasica* Berg, which is over 10 cm long and has a gold-gleaming body with no conspicuous spots on the sides, inhabits the

Sabanejewia aurata

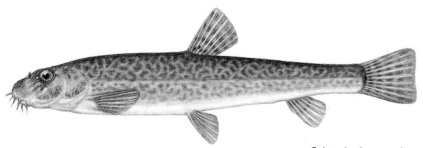

Sabanejewia caucasica

rivers Kuban, Terek, Kuma and Sulak in the Caucasus. The last European spined loach, *S. conspersa* Cantoni, lives in the rivers of northern Italy and has a cylindrical, brownish body with a violet lustre.

Little is known of the mode of life of these small loaches, because they lead a very secretive existence and are nowhere particularly abundant.

All spined loaches are short-lived, with a life span of only 3—4 years. Spawning usually takes place in April and May and the females lay a relatively small number of eggs (a few hundred), which they deposit on sand and stones on the bed, in flowing water.

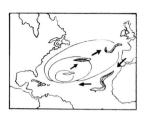

Spawning grounds and development of the larvae of *A. anguilla*

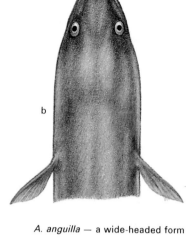

A. anguilla — a wide-headed form

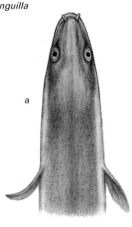

A. anguilla — a narrow-headed form

European Eel
Anguilla anguilla (L.)

● ○ ■
Eels
Anguillidae

The European Eel has a long, serpentine body almost circular in cross section. Its dorsal and anal fin are continuous with the caudal fin and the only paired fins are the pectorals. The small, oval scales are deeply embedded in the skin. The lateral line is properly developed. The mouth, which ends below the eyes, is the terminal type and there are always teeth in the jaws. The opercula terminate just ahead of the pectoral fins. The European Eel has a dark greyish green back, lighter sides and a greyish white belly; after it reaches sexual maturity, its sides and belly are silvery. Male eels are never more than about 50 cm long, but the females measure up to 150 cm and exceptionally weigh over 6 kg. Dur-

ing the eels' spawning migration to the Sargasso Sea, their eyes grow strikingly larger; the same phenomenon is encountered in eels kept many years in captivity without any opportunity of escaping. One such eel lived 68 years in a pool on the premises of a Prague insurance company and its eyes grew larger just before it died; the evidence is deposited in the National Museum in Prague.

The European Eel lives in fresh water throughout the whole of Europe, where it is a typical bottom-dwelling fish. Adult eels migrate downstream to the sea on dark, moonless nights and head for their spawning grounds north of the Bermudas, where, about one and a half

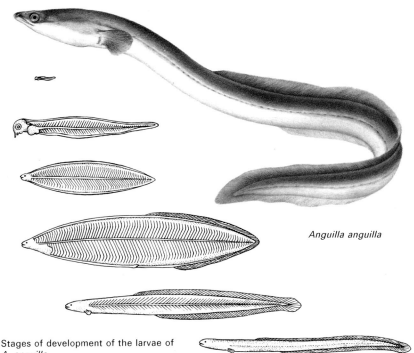

Anguilla anguilla

Stages of development of the larvae of
A. anguilla

years after setting out on their journey, they spawn in deep water and then die. The transparent little larvae, which look like willow leaves, drift with the Gulf Stream towards the coast of Europe, reaching it in about three years. Between October and April, in river mouths, they develop into elvers measuring about 6 cm, which migrate upstream, deep inland, in huge masses. During their migration they overcome the most diverse obstacles (rock faces, waterfalls and often dry land) until they finally find a place to settle and then remain there 13—16 years. They spend the winters in the mud on the river bed.

Eels begin to acquire scales in about their fifth year in fresh water, when they measure 16—18 cm. Their age can be determined from the structure of the scales and from the increments on the vertebrae. Two ecological forms of the European Eel exist—a narrow-headed form (a) and a wide-headed form (b)—according to their feeding habits. Narrow-headed eels (probably males) live largely on very small creatures (insect larvae, worms, etc) and wide-headed eels (probably females) mainly on small fish.

The European Eel is a commercially important fish. It is caught in special eel-baskets, with various types of nets and with long night-lines and is particularly popular with anglers. The elvers are caught in vast quantities off the European coast and are then transported inland, where they are placed in fish ponds and open waters. The adult Eels are caught as they migrate seawards; smoked, they are regarded as a very great delicacy.

Distribution of
S. glanis (blue)
and *S. aristotelis* (red)

European Catfish; Wels
Silurus glanis L.

○ ■
Freshwater catfishes
Siluridae

The European Catfish, one of the biggest fishes in European waters, has a long, scaleless body, a large head and a huge mouth surrounded by three pairs of fleshy barbels—two long ones on the upper jaw and four shorter ones on the lower jaw. The dorsal fin is small and soft, with 3—5 rays, while the anal fin is extremely long and stretches backwards from the anus until it almost touches the rounded caudal fin. The tail is very long and the part of the body from the anus to the end of the caudal fin accounts for three fifths of total body length (the anterior part of the body for only two fifths). The eyes are small and the anterior nostrils terminate in short, fleshy tubes. Colouring depends on the environment; the back is usually dark to almost black, sometimes with a greenish, bluish or brownish tinge, the sides are a dingy yellowish white, generally with distinct greyish brown marbling, and the light, greyish white belly is marked with dark spots of varying sizes. Not infrequently we come across red-eyed albino specimens among normally coloured catfish.

In European waters this fish grows to a length of over two metres and weighs over 100 kg. It lives in big, deep rivers and has a predilection for deep dams. In Europe it is distributed eastwards from the catchment area of the Rhine and in the north as far as the most southerly part of Sweden and Finland. It does not inhabit the rivers flowing into the Arctic Ocean or south European rivers emptying into the western part of the Mediterranean.

If it has sufficient food, the European Catfish grows very quickly and by the time it is nine years old weighs 12—16 kg; adult Catfish have considerable annual weight increments. European Catfish spawn in May and June, at water temperatures of over 18 °C, in shallow water overgrown with aquatic vegetation. The eggs are laid in a kind of untidy nest prepared by the female; the male then fertilizes them and stands guard over them and the newly hatched fry. The latter at first look like tadpoles; they have no barbels and do not begin to resemble the adults for about ten days. Their first food consists of small crustaceans and worms, etc; adult catfish live mainly on fish (chiefly tiny species), but also catch frogs, small mammals, large Roach and Bream and even water birds.

The economic importance of the European Catfish is particularly great in the Black Sea region. In recent years this fish has frequently been introduced into carp ponds as a secondary predator. In central and eastern Europe it is regarded as a great trophy by anglers, who catch it with live fish, spoon lures or worms.

Aristotle's Catfish, *Silurus aristotelis* (Agassiz), a related species, lives in the river Akhelóos in Greece.

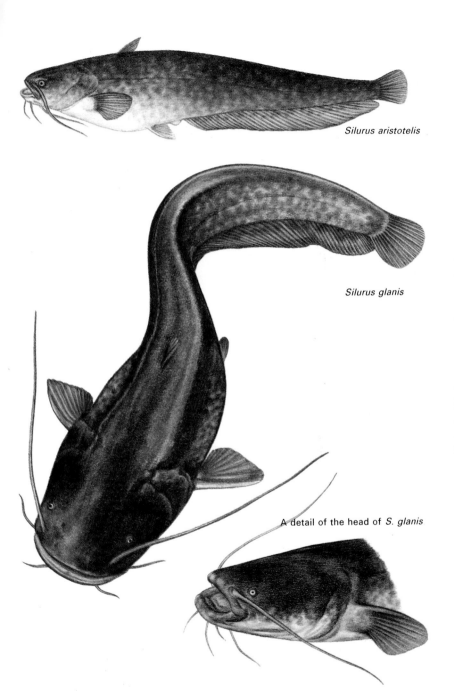

Silurus aristotelis

Silurus glanis

A detail of the head of *S. glanis*

147

Distribution of *I. nebulosus*

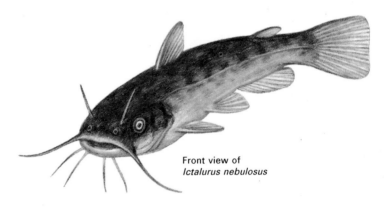

Front view of
Ictalurus nebulosus

Horned Pout; American Catfish
Ictalurus nebulosus LE SUEUR

American freshwater catfishes
Ictaluridae

The Horned Pout, a North American relative of the European Catfish, was imported into Europe at the end of the last century. It differs from the European species in two main respects—the small adipose fin behind the dorsal fin and the larger number of barbels (four on each jaw). The longest barbels are those at the corners of the mouth on the upper jaw; the two shorter ones in front of the nostrils point upwards. In its dorsal fin and pectoral fins the Horned Pout has sharp erectile spines; it uses these to defend itself and if the fish is handled they can cause painful injuries which take a long time to heal. The Horned Pout is plainly coloured; its back is brownish green or dark grey, its sides are lighter, with a golden sheen, and are sometimes discernibly mottled, its belly is greyish white (at spawning time yellowish or faintly orange) and its barbels are grey to almost black.

In Europe the Horned Pout was introduced into fishponds, from which it subsequently spread to many rivers. The limits of its present distribution in Europe are very uncertain. It lives over a relatively large range, but only in pockets. It does not occur in the Iberian

Ictalurus nebulosus

peninsula, southern Italy, the western Balkans and the rivers flowing into the Arctic Ocean.

The Horned Pout likes the deep, quieter parts of rivers, where it frequents the bed. It is active mainly in the evening and at night. When small, it lives on zooplankton and the larvae of midges and other insects, but its food often includes larger morsels and vegetation. In Europe it grows to a length of only 25—30 cm and weighs about 0.5 kg, but in its original home in the northern parts of the USA and in Canada it usually measures up to 45 cm and sometimes weighs over 2 kg. It becomes sexually mature in its second or third year.

The Horned Pout spawns in May and June. The eggs are laid in shallow, overgrown backwaters, where the female builds a nest on a sandy bed. The male guards the eggs and the newly hatched fry, which remain together in a shoal. In European waters, the Horned Pout measures 18—24 cm by its fourth year; it grows faster in fishponds and rivers than it does in pools, river arms and irrigation canals.

The hopes placed by fishermen in importation of the Horned Pout into European waters have been disappointed and it has not turned out to be a profitable fish. At one time it was kept in ponds, but today it no longer plays a role in intensive large-scale fish production. It is caught to a limited extent by anglers, who mostly use worms as bait. The Horned Pout is very voracious and in places where it is abundant it drives virtually all other species away. It has very savoury and characteristically orange-coloured flesh.

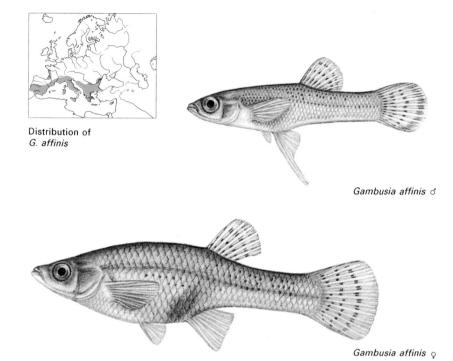

Distribution of
G. affinis

Gambusia affinis ♂

Gambusia affinis ♀

Mediterranean Toothcarp
Aphanius fasciatus (Humboldt et Valenciennes)
Tooth carps
Cyprinodontidae

The Mosquito Fish was brought to European fresh waters from the southern parts of the USA, to help combat malaria. It is a tiny fish, the males measuring only about 35 mm and the females not more than 60 mm. Its general colour is greyish to bluish and it has a translucent body. Its back is olive brown, its sides are lighter and its belly is white. The caudal fin is rounded and the anal fin, in the males, has been converted to an organ of copulation (a gonopodium). The eyes are crossed by a dark stripe and the mouth is distinctly dorsal.

This fish occurs in warm fresh and brackish waters of southern Europe, from Portugal, Spain and the southwest of France across Italy and the Balkan countries to the southern parts of the USSR. It is ovoviviparous and the female gives birth to up to 80 young three to five times a year. Its diet consists mainly of insects and their larvae, particularly the larvae of mosquitoes which transmit malaria. We can come across this species in brooks, small pools, rivers and their estuaries and, in some places, in thermal springs with a temperature of over 40 °C (in southwestern Bulgaria).

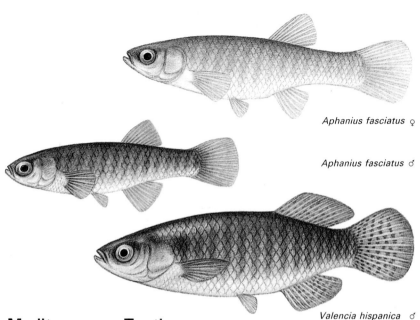

Aphanius fasciatus ♀

Aphanius fasciatus ♂

Valencia hispanica ♂

Mediterranean Toothcarp
Aphanius fasciatus (HUMBOLDT ET VALENCIENNES)

Tooth carps
Cyprinodontidae

The most widespread original European member of the family Cyprinodontidae is the Mediterranean Toothcarp which occurs in fresh and brackish water in the Mediterranean region, from the south of France to Asia Minor and Cyprus, on the European Mediterranean islands and probably in North Africa as well. The males of this species are differently coloured from the females; the male has a greyish blue body, marked with 10—15 dark cross bands, and yellow fins, while the female has indistinct stripes and pale grey fins. Spawning takes place throughout the whole of the warm season; the female lays the eggs on aquatic vegetation, the male fertilizes them and the fry are hatched in about 14 days. The fish live on aquatic invertebrates, débris and parts of plants.

The related Spanish Killifish or Iberian Toothcarp, *A. iberus* (Cuvier et Valenciennes), which lives on the coast of southern and eastern Spain, has a bluish green or bright blue body with an olive green back and a white belly. It has about 15 narrow, light blue cross stripes on its sides and dark spots on its fins.

The last of the European species, the Valencia Toothcarp, *Valencia hispanica* (Cuvier et Valenciennes), lives in fresh and brackish water in the south and west of Spain, on the island of Kérkira (Corfu) and in Albania. It grows to a length of 7—8 cm and has a flat-sided body. The males are brown, with a metallic lustre, and have a yellowish white belly; their scales are dark-edged. Above the pectoral fins, behind the opercula, there is a large dark spot and dark cross bands are present on the sides.

Tooth carps are of significance only as aquarium fishes.

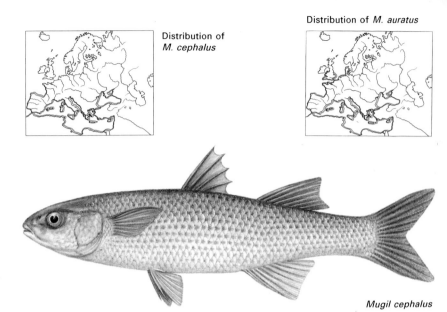

Mugil cephalus

Striped Grey Mullet
Mugil cephalus L.

○ ▷
Mullets
Mugilidae

The marine mullet family includes a few species which regularly visit estuaries and often migrate long distances up the relevant rivers. The first one, the Striped Grey Mullet, is about 70 cm long, with an elongate, slightly flat-sided body, a flat-topped head, a small mouth, large scales and a discontinuous lateral line. Like other members of the family it has two dorsal fins—a short anterior fin with four spiny rays and a markedly posteriorly situated second fin in which only the first two rays are spiny and the rest are soft. Its eyes have a large, well developed adipose lid. Its back is ash grey, with a golden and blue sheen, and there are nine or ten narrow dark stripes along its sides. The opercula have a gold and silver lustre. The Striped Grey Mullet is distributed along the European coast from the mouth of the Loire to the Sea of Azov and the Black Sea.

The fish swim in shoals. They are excellent swimmers and leapers. They spawn in the spring, in the sea and in river mouths. The eggs have a drop of oil enabling them to float in the water. The adult fish live on crustaceans, worms, small molluscs and similar creatures in the mud, which they crush with their pharyngeal teeth. Like other grey mullets they are economically valuable fish; they are caught with lines and with nets.

Among related grey mullets which regularly invade European rivers from the sea, mention should be made of the Common Grey Mullet, *Mugil labeo* Cuvier, which grows to a length of up to 20 cm, the Thick-lipped Mullet, *M. labrosus* Risso, which measures 30—50 cm, and the Sharpnose Mullet, *M. saliens* Risso, which is about 40 cm long. All three are common along European coasts and all are economically important fishes.

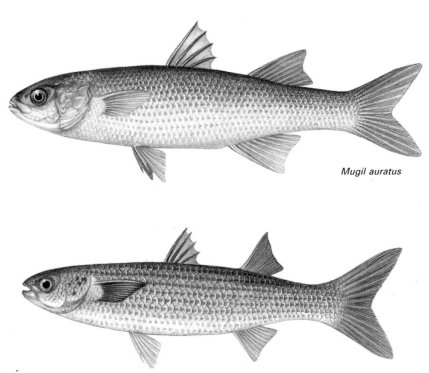

Mugil auratus

Mugil saliens

Golden Grey Mullet
Mugil (Liza) auratus Riso

○ ▷
Mullets
Mugilidae

The Golden Grey Mullet, which grows to a length of about 50 cm, is one of the larger mullets that invade European rivers from the sea. It has a brownish back, 6—7 narrow dark brown stripes along its sides and a silvery white belly. Behind each eye it has a striking golden spot and another, similar one on each operculum. The mouth is larger than in other mullets and the upper jaw is armed with teeth. The transparent gelatinous lids are rudimentary. The biology and economic significance of this species conform to the data for other mullets.

The Thin-lipped Grey Mullet, *M. capito* Cuvier, which is distributed from the coast of southern Norway to the Black Sea and has a resident freshwater population in Lake Shkodër (Scutari) in south-western Yugoslavia, has a shorter and thicker snout. Its back is brownish grey, with a metallic lustre, there are 6—7 dark stripes along its sides and its belly is white. It measures up to about 50 cm and lives in large shoals.

All grey mullets have very tasty flesh and therefore hold an important position in the European coastal fishing industry in the Atlantic, the Mediterranean and the Black Sea.

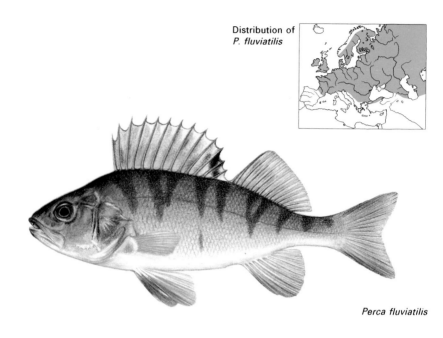

Distribution of
P. fluviatilis

Perca fluviatilis

Perch
Perca fluviatilis L.

○ ■
Perches
Percidae

The Perch has a high-backed, flat-sided body, which in water rich in nutrients is often strikingly arched. At the base of the back of its spiny first dorsal fin the Perch has a conspicuous black spot. The opercula terminate in a large spine and the anterior opercular bone has a toothed, saw-like edge. The scales, which are relatively small, are of the ctenoid type and are embedded deep in the skin. The lateral line ends just before reaching the base of the caudal fin. The mouth is large and the upper jaw stretches to below the eyes. The dark back and lighter grey sides are crossed by 5—9 black bands. Perch are very variably coloured, in correlation to their environment; brightly marked Perch from the lower parts of trout streams are particularly handsome; Perch from deep water are usually very dark and their cross bands are frequently indistinct. The first dorsal fin is grey, the second is translucent and greenish yellow. The pectoral fins are yellowish, the ventral fins and anal fin reddish and the caudal fin is a shade of red. In Europe, the Perch usually measures 30—50 cm and weighs about 1—2 kg.

The Perch's European range extends from Great Britain to the river Ural and in Asia it stretches eastwards as far as the river Kolyma. It is absent from the west of Scandinavia, Scotland, Portugal, Spain, Italy and the western part of the Balkan peninsula.

The Perch spawns in April and May and sometimes continues into June. The eggs are joined together in ribbon-like strings 1—2 m long and 1—2 cm

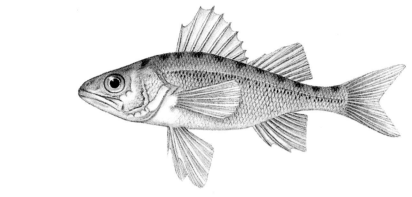

Percarina demidoffi

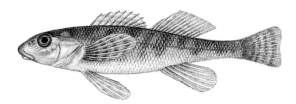

Romanichthys valsanicola

wide; they are laid on stones, submerged branches and roots or aquatic plants in shallow water, generally at night. The parents do not look after either the eggs or the fry, which usually hatch in 14—17 days. The newly hatched young fish is 3—6 mm long and has an egg-shaped yolk sac with a large drop of oil, enabling it to float in the water.

The fry at first live on small planktonic organisms and later on the fry of other (especially cyprinid) fishes; the adults live mainly on fish. Young Perch often form large shoals and sometimes drive prey towards one another. Young Perch hunt in shallow water; older fish prefer deep water and solitude.

Where it occurs in large numbers, the Perch is an economically important fish. It is caught with various types of drag-nets, drop-nets and gill nets. It is very popular with anglers, who employ different animal baits and spoon lures and catch it chiefly in lakes and dams, where it grows to a considerable size.

The mouths of the Dnestr, Dnepr and Bug in the USSR are inhabited by the related *Percarina demidoffi* Nordmann, which grows to a mere 7—10 cm in length; it forms huge shoals which frequent both fresh water and sea water and is an important component of the diet of the Pike-perch. In 1957, another member of the perch family, *Romanichthys valsanicola* Dumitrescu et Banarescu, was discovered in Romanian tributaries of the Danube coming from the eastern Carpathians; this fish measures over 12 cm and inhabits the trout and grayling zones of rushing mountain rivers.

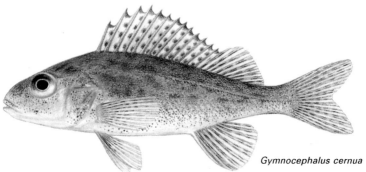

Gymnocephalus cernua

Ruffe; Pope
Gymnocephalus cernua (L.)

Perches
Percidae

The members of the genus *Gymnocephalus* are small fish with a perch-like body, but whereas the Perch has two separate dorsal fins, in these fish the first, spiny dorsal fin and the second, soft dorsal fin are joined together in one. The Ruffe measures only 10—15 cm (exceptionally a little more). It has a greyish green or brownish grey back marked with indistinct black spots, lighter brown sides and a yellowish white, dark-spotted belly. Its opercula have a striking metallic lustre. Its greyish brown dorsal and caudal fins are thickly speckled with small dark spots; its ventral fins and anal fin are dingy yellow to greyish red.

In Europe, the Ruffe's range stretches eastwards from England and the north of France far beyond the Urals; it does not live in Ireland, Scotland, western and northern Norway, the Iberian peninsula, Italy or the southern parts of the Balkans. It inhabits the lower reaches of rivers with a sandy bed and shuns water with dense aquatic vegetation. It frequents deep water and does not like strong currents. The winter is spent in deep pools and during the warm part of the year it lives in small or large shoals. In April and May it spawns in shallow water, laying the eggs in bands on the bed, on roots and on submerged branches. The young live on minute planktonic and benthic food, larger specimens on the larvae of aquatic insects, worms, the eggs of other fishes and similar titbits. The Ruffe grows very slowly and does not measure 10 cm until it is about four or five years old.

In 1974, the related species *G. baloni* Holčik et Hensel was described in the Danube. Little is known of this fish's biology, but it appears to live in water with a faster current than the Ruffe does.

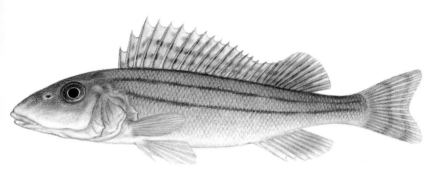

Gymnocephalus schraetzer

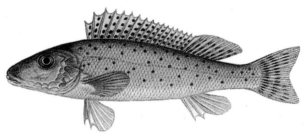

Gymnocephalus acerina

Striped Ruffe; Schraetzer
Gymnocephalus schraetzer (L.)

Perches
Percidae

The Striped Ruffe, which grows to a length of 15—20 cm (occasionally 25 cm), inhabits the Danube and its tributaries. It differs from the two preceding species in respect of its colouring, since it has a dark olive green back and yellow sides and on either side it has three or four longitudinal (sometimes discontinuous) black stripes. On the anterior part of its dorsal fin it has regular rows of dark oval spots.

The Striped Ruffe lives in small shoals in deep water with a strong current over a hard bed. It spawns from March to May; the eggs, which are strung together in ribbons, are laid on stones and roots in flowing water. The fish have a predilection for deep pools hollowed out by the current, where they catch food (mainly insect larvae, worms, small fry and fish eggs) together in shoals. At spawning time large shoals invade the tributaries of the Danube.

The similar species *G. acerina* (Güld.), which measures about 15 cm, inhabits the rivers flowing into the northern part of the Black Sea and the Sea of Azov; it lives in fast-flowing water.

157

Zingel zingel

Zingel
Zingel zingel (L.)

Perches
Percidae

The genus *Zingel* is represented in Europe by three species. The largest, which is about half a metre long and weighs up to 1 kg, is a long, slim-bodied fish with only slightly flattened sides and a flat-topped head. Its head is partly covered with scales and has a ventral mouth. The Zingel has a shorter caudal segment than the related Streber. It has a yellowish brown, dark-spotted body, with four dark cross bands (often indistinct) on the sides. It lives in the basins of the Danube, the Dnestr and the Prut.

It spawns in April and in May and generally sticks the eggs to stones in a gentle current or in shallow water. The fish itself frequents the main channel of

big rivers, where it can find adequate shelter under stones. It lives on benthic invertebrates, supplemented in the spawning season by the eggs of other fishes. In some places, in certain reservoirs in the valleys of the Danube basin, its numbers have distinctly increased.

The species *Zingel asper* (L.), which measures 15—22 cm, inhabits the basin of the Rhône; like the other members of the genus it is a largely nocturnal fish and lives on benthic fauna. It spawns from March to April. This fish is differently coloured from the Danubian Zingel species and has a light brown or greyish body with three irregular dark stripes on its rear end.

Distribution of
Z. streber

Zingel streber

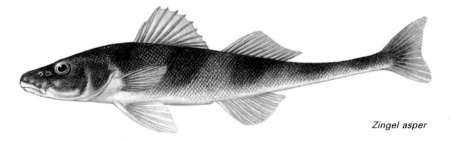

Zingel asper

Streber
Zingel streber (Siebold)

Perches
Percidae

The Streber can be distinguished from the two preceding species by its very long, thin tail. Its back and sides are marked with four or five vivid oblique black stripes. Its ground colour is yellowish brown; its belly is always lighter than its sides. There are no scales on the front of the belly. It grows to a length of 15 cm (exceptionally up to 20 cm). In Europe it is endemic to the Danube and its tributaries, from the delta as far as Bavaria; the subspecies *Z. streber balcanicus* has been described in the river Vardar in the Balkans.

In the spawning season, i.e. in March

and April, the Streber's body acquires a metallic lustre and a spawning rash appears on the head of both the male and the female. The Streber is more sensitive to pollution of the water and requires more oxygen than the other two species and it therefore occurs in the submontane parts of the rivers, where it frequents shallow water with a sandy or gravelly bed. It lives on benthic invertebrates and is active chiefly at night. It grows very slowly and takes four years to reach a length of about 15 cm.

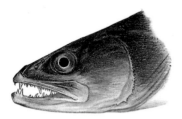

A detail of the head of *S. lucioperca*

Distribution of *S. lucioperca*

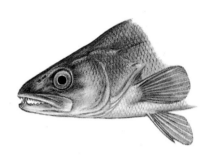

A detail of the head of *S. marinus*

Pike-perch
Stizostedion lucioperca (L.)

○ ■
Perches
Percidae

Pike-perch can always be differentiated from the Perch by the relatively large space between their dorsal fins (in the Perch they are close together) and their elongate, fusiform body, which is never so strikingly arched behind the head as it is in the Perch.

The most widespread European member of this genus is the Pike-perch, a robust fish up to more than 1 m long and weighing over 10 kg. It has a greyish brown or greyish green back and light, silvery green sides marked with 8—12 blackish brown cross stripes which frequently break up into spots. On the dorsal fins and the caudal fin, between the rays, there are rows of small dark spots;

the other fins are greyish yellow (the pectoral fins pale yellow). In the spawning season the males have a blue-marbled belly, the females a pure white belly. In Europe, the Pike-perch is distributed eastwards from the Rhine to the Baltic, the Black Sea, the Sea of Azov and the Caspian Sea regions. With the exception of southeastern England, it does not live in western Europe and neither does it occur on the south European peninsulas or in the northern parts of Scandinavia and the USSR.

The Pike-perch frequents deep, quiet water. It generally stays in hiding during the daytime and goes hunting in the evening and early morning. It is ex-

160

Stizostedion lucioperca

tremely sensitive to oxygen deficiency and to pollution of the water. It spawns in April and May, in shallow water with a temperature of over 6 °C. The male makes a kind of rough nest on the bed, uncovering the rootlets of aquatic plants so that the female can attach the eggs to them. The male protects the nest; it fans the fertilized eggs with its fins to keep them free from mud and other alluvial matter and to ensure a constant supply of clean, oxygenated water; it also guards the fry for a short time. Young Pike-perch consort in shoals. At first they live on plankton and small insects, but when they measure 3—4 cm they begin to catch the fry of cyprinid fishes, which by then are just beginning to leave the eggs. Adult Pike-perch live virtually entirely on fish. They never hunt such big prey as Pike do, however, and can therefore be kept in carp ponds together with young carp.

In suitable ponds, pond-keepers provide Pike-perch with nests made of sedge rootlets and after the fish have spawned they pack the nests in moss and ice and dispatch them, sometimes for quite long distances, for transplantation to open water. The transplantation of year-old pond-bred Pike-perch to rivers and dams yields better results, however.

The north-western part of the Black Sea and the Caspian Sea are inhabited by the closely related *Stizostedion marinus* Cuvier et Valenciennes, which at spawning time migrates up the Bug and the tributary rivers of the southern part of the Caspian Sea. It grows to a length of about 60 cm and has more scales on its head than the Pike-perch. It lives mainly on gobies and herring.

These pike-perches are both economically important fish and are very popular with anglers.

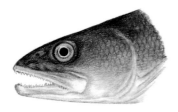

A detail of the head of *S. volgense*

Distribution of *S. volgense*

Stizostedion volgense

East European Pike-perch;
Volga Pike-perch
Stizostedion volgense (GMELIN)

○ ■
Perches
Percidae

The East European Pike-Perch, which is closely related to the two preceding species, is smaller than they are, with a probable maximum length and weight of 45 cm and 1.5 kg respectively. It is immediately distinguishable from the Pike-perch by its teeth; the latter has a few teeth much longer than the rest in the front of its jaws, while the teeth of the East European Pike-perch are all the same size. The East European Pike-perch closely resembles the Pike-Perch in form and colouring, but the 5—7 dark cross stripes on its sides never break up into spots, as they frequently do in the other species. The opercula of the East European Pike-perch are covered with scales and there are 70—83 scales in its lateral line (in the Pike-perch 55—77).

The biology of the two species is also similar. The East European Pike-perch reaches adulthood in its third to fourth year. It spawns in April and May, in places with a muddy bed and an adequate amount of aquatic plants. Initially it lives on small planktonic and benthic animals; the adults catch fish, but they also live on small aquatic creatures and on insects which have fallen into the water. They continue feeding even in the coldest winter months.

The East European Pike-perch occurs in the northern tributary rivers of the Black Sea, the Sea of Azov and the Caspian Sea. It swims up the Danube as far as Vienna and up its big tributaries.

A ctenoid scale

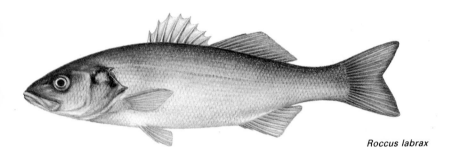

Roccus labrax

Sea Bass
Roccus (Dicentrarchus) labrax (L.)

The Sea Bass, a member of the sea-perch family Serranidae, and a relative of the European perches, frequently invades fresh water. Like perches, it has two dorsal fins, but has three hard, sharp-pointed rays in its anal fin (perches only two). It has a dark grey back, lighter sides with a silvery sheen, a white belly, a black lateral line and a distinctive dark, blackish grey spot on the inner upper edge of its opercula. It grows to a length of about 1 m and a weight of up to 12 kg.

It often forms shoals in the region of estuaries and invades the rivers themselves. In the winter it retires to deep water. It is distributed along the Euro-

pean shores of the Atlantic from the north of Norway to Gibraltar and it also occurs in the Mediterranean, the Adriatic and the Black Sea. It lives as a resident freshwater fish in Lake Shkodër (L. Scutari) in southern Yugoslavia, near the Adriatic coast, and in the river Nile in North Africa.

It spawns in estuaries from May to August; the eggs have a drop of oil which keeps them floating in the water. *R. labrax* is a predator feeding mainly on sea fish which live in shoals, such as herring, sardines and anchovies. As an economically important and highly prized fish, it is caught with the most diverse types of nets and by anglers.

163

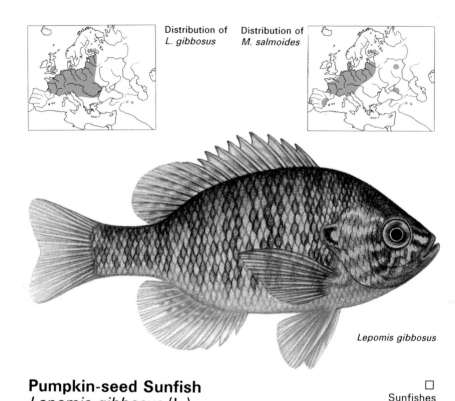

Distribution of
L. gibbosus

Distribution of
M. salmoides

Lepomis gibbosus

Pumpkin-seed Sunfish
Lepomis gibbosus (L.)

Sunfishes
Centrarchidae

Originally inhabitants of North America, three species of sunfishes were brought to Europe in the 1890's. Only two still live in European waters.

The Pumpkin-seed Sunfish was imported because of its decorative appearance; it was soon a very popular fish in aquaria and here and there it was set free in open water, where, if conditions were favourable, it reproduced and spread to rivers and ponds. It has a high-backed, deep-bellied, flat-sided discoid body and a small mouth. Its back is olive green and its gleaming bluish sides are covered with vivid round, reddish or orange-coloured spots; the tapering process at the end of each operculum is adorned with a similarly conspicuous spot. Luminous blue and orange stripes are present on the sides of the head. In Europe, the Pumpkin-seed Sunfish usually grows to an average length of only 15 cm. In some places—mainly in central and southern Europe—it is fairly widespread.

The Pumpkin-seed Sunfish spawns from May to August in shallow nests made in sand; the males guard the eggs and the fry. The fry live largely on plankton, bigger specimens on bottom-dwelling creatures, insect imagos and small fish. Here and there this is an abundant species in fishponds, riverside pools and irrigation canals and it also occurs in many European rivers. Its economic siginificance in Europe is virtually nil.

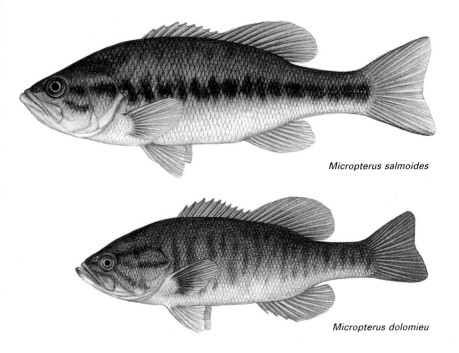

Micropterus salmoides

Micropterus dolomieu

Largemouth Black Bass
Micropterus salmoides (LACÉPÈDE)

□
Sunfishes
Centrarchidae

The Largemouth Black Bass is a robust, not particularly high-backed fish with a large mouth stretching to the posterior corner of its eyes. It generally has a dark green back, silvery sides and a silvery green belly. Along its sides runs an undulating dark stripe, which often disappears in big fish. In Europe the Largemouth Black Bass measures up to 30—35 cm and weighs 1—2 kg. In its original home, in the southern USA, it may exceptionally weigh as much as 10 kg.

It is kept in European fishponds as a secondary fish and has also been introduced into a number of lakes in the Austrian Alps, but has become established in only a few places. Attempts to introduce it to various lakes in the USSR have proved successful.

The Largemouth Black Bass reaches sexual maturity in its third or fourth years. It spawns in May and June. The male builds the nest and guards both the eggs and—for a short time—the fry. Young bass live on planktonic organisms, adult specimens on small fish and benthic fauna; in the spring they particularly enjoy tadpoles. In European waters the Largemouth Black Bass does not grow so fast as it does in America and is therefore not regarded as a promising fish for the fishing industry.

The related species *Micropterus dolomieu* Lacépède, which was imported together with the Largemouth Black Bass, failed to become established in most of the places where it was introduced.

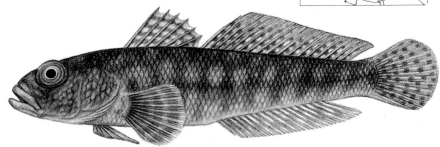

Gobius ophiocephalus

Snakehead Goby; Grass Goby
Gobius ophiocephalus (PALLAS)

▷
Gobies
Gobiidae

Almost twenty species of marine gobies are to be found in European rivers and streams, especially near where these flow into the sea. Some have become adapted to life in fresh water so well that they occur in both a marine and a resident freshwater form.

Gobies are sturdy little benthic fish living mostly in coastal water and seldom in the open sea. They have two dorsal fins—a short, spiny fin in front and a long one behind, in which, as in the anal fin, only the first ray is spiny. The caudal fin is more or less rounded, while the ventral fins, which are situated far anteriorly, are fused to form a suctorial device giving the fish a firm hold on the sea bed in the breaker zone or in a strong current. Gobies often display sexual dimorphism.

The Snakehead Goby, which inhabits the Mediterranean, the Black Sea, the Sea of Azov and their tributary rivers, measures about 25 cm and is one of the larger gobies. Compared with others it has a relatively tapering and high head. Its body is brown, with dark mottling, and there are white spots on the sides of its head and at the base of its pectoral fins. The first dorsal fin is marked with three pairs of longitudinal brown stripes and a round dark brown spot is present at the base of its caudal fin.

The Snakehead Goby frequents shallow sea water with plenty of seaweed. Here it builds a nest—mostly in April—and spawns.

The Black-spotted Goby (*G. melanostomus* Pallas), which is about 20 cm long, is of local economic significance in the coastal waters of the Black Sea, the Sea of Azov and their tributary rivers, where it is also important as food for bigger marine fishes.

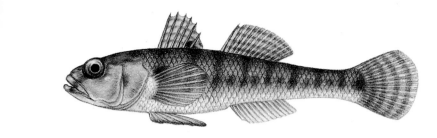

Pomatoschistus microps

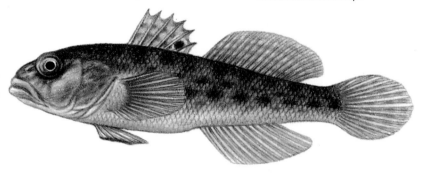

Gobius melanostomus

Common Goby
Pomatoschistus microps (Kröyer)

The Common Goby, which is only some 5 cm long and is one of the smaller gobies, lives along European coasts from the Black Sea and the Mediterranean as far north as the middle of the Scandinavian coast; in the Baltic it reaches Stockholm in the north and Rügen in the east.

Its body is basically sandy yellow to greyish yellow and its sides are decorated with a row of irregular black spots, which often blend to form narrow cross bars. There are dark stripes between the eyes and the corners of the mouth and similar stripes between the nostrils and the lower lip. At spawning time the males have a dark blue spot at the back of their dorsal fin and their anal fin, throat and opercula are black.

The Common Goby lives in shoals on a sandy bed in shallows in the sea and in fresh water near the coast; it often buries itself in the sand. Its diet consists mainly of small planktonic and benthic organisms.

P. canestrini (Ninni) is a similar, closely related freshwater fish occurring in fresh water in Yugoslavia and in the region round Venice. The base of its tail, the top of its head and its chin are black.

167

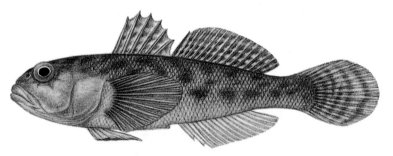

Gobius fluviatilis

River Goby
Gobius fluviatilis PALLAS

Gobies
Gobiidae

As its name implies, the River Goby is to be found chiefly in fresh water. It inhabits rivers flowing into the Black Sea, is about 20 cm long and differs from other gobies by the shape of its second dorsal fin, which slopes noticeably downwards towards the tail. It has a relatively wide head and a brownish, dark-spotted back and its dorsal fins are both marked with longitudinal rows of dark spots forming a pattern of stripes.

The River Goby inhabits the lower and middle reaches of the Danube and its tributaries, the lower and middle Dnestr, Bug and Dnepr, the Crimea re-gion and the rivers emptying into the northern part of the Caspian Sea.

It is a bottom-dwelling fish and in April, like most other male gobies, the male builds a nest on the river bed and guards the eggs. This species lives mainly on small benthic invertebrates, such as insect larvae and crustaceans.

Several other gobies are distributed in the region of the Black Sea, the Caspian Sea, the Sea of Azov and the Aral Sea; large species are economically important and are caught with various types of nets and with rod and line.

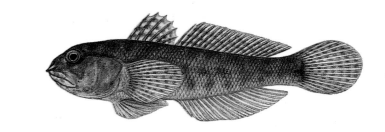

Proterorhinus marmoratus

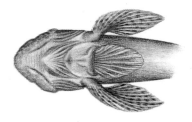

View of the underside of the body of
P. marmoratus

Mottled Black Sea Goby
Proterorhinus marmoratus PALLAS

▷
Gobies
Gobiidae

This small goby measuring 7—11 cm comes from the Black Sea, the Sea of Azov and their tributary rivers. As in all gobies, its ventral fins are fused to form a suctorial disc. Its anterior nostrils, which lie above the mouth, are like short tubes. Its ground colour is greyish brown, with a few dark transverse spots on the sides and a more or less distinct dark, light-bordered triangular spot at the base of the tail; the fins are marked with fine brown speckles.

This species lives in salt, brackish and fresh water, and in rivers is to be found a very long way upstream—in the Danube, for instance, as far as the place where this river is joined by the Morava; it also inhabits the Bug, the Dnepr, the rivers flowing into the Sea of Azov and perhaps the river Maritza as well.

The Mottled Black Sea Goby frequents the bed of gently flowing and stagnant water with an abundance of water weeds. It usually spawns in April and May and lives on small aquatic insect larvae and other small benthic animals. Since it can tolerate a mild degree of pollution, there are many places where it is relatively common. It also occurs behind the stone dam in the mainstream of the Danube, where it finds sufficient shelter, and lives in relatively fast-flowing irrigation canals in southern Slovakia and in overgrown meanders along the course of the Danube.

Unfortunately, we have no detailed information on the biology of the Mottled Black Sea Goby.

Blennius fluviatilis ♂

Blennius fluviatilis ♀

River Blenny; Freshwater Blenny
Blennius fluviatilis Asso

Blennies are small fish which can often be encountered in shallow water along rocky European coasts. Some of them have striking outgrowths above their eyes, others wear a kind of helmet, while many are beautifully and distinctively coloured and are therefore popular in marine aquaria (like *Blennius pavo*, depicted here, or *B. sphinx*). Many of these marine blennies have a habit of climbing out of the water on to the rocks. At spawning time the males defend their territory against rivals and conscientiously care for their future offspring.

The only blenny to be found in fresh water in Europe is the River Blenny,

a small fish usually about 10 cm (seldom up to 15 cm) long, with an elongate body and thick skin with rudimentary scales deeply embedded in it. The River Blenny has a very long dorsal fin, which starts just behind the head above the beginning of the lateral line, terminates just before reaching the rounded caudal fin and is the same height throughout. The small mouth is armed with a row of teeth and in each jaw there is one large, curved tooth. There are small fleshy excrescences above the eyes and on the crown of the head there is a low fleshy crest which is more strongly developed in the males than in the females. The River Blenny has an olive brown back,

Blennius pavo

lighter sides and a yellowish white belly. Its back and sides are decorated with dark brown spots or streaks and there are also dark spots on its dorsal fin; two or three distinctive brown stripes are often present on its cheeks. The colouring of individual populations varies considerably with the environmental conditions. This Blenny is distributed in the sea and in fresh water in the Mediterranean region, eastwards from southern and eastern Spain and the south of France across Corsica, Sardinia, Sicily and Italy to Cyprus and Asia Minor.

The river Blenny lives both in coastal waters of the Mediterranean and in lakes, slow-flowing streams and canals with a low water column and clean water. When young it often forms large shoals; older fish live solitarily under stones and in various other shelters on the bottom and near the edge. They live on bottom-dwelling invertebrate animals.

In the spawning season, the male River Blenny looks for a convenient hollow under a stone, which it cleans and defends vigorously against all other males. When the fight has been won, the whole of its body turns almost black. It then peeps out of the nest and with weaving movements of its body it lures a female to come in and attach its eggs to the ceiling of the cavern. Finally, it fertilizes the eggs and guards them against enemies. By wriggling its body and fanning the eggs with its pectoral fins, it ensures that its future offspring have a continuous supply of fresh oxygenated water; it also removes any dead eggs from the nest. At a temperature of about 20 °C the fry hatch in roughly 14 days.

171

Cottus gobio

Miller's Thumb; Bullhead
Cottus gobio L.

▶
Bullheads, Sculpins
Cottidae

The Miller's Thumb is a small fish with a large, wide, flat-topped head and a large mouth, which lives at the bottom of clean mountain and submontane rivers and streams. Having an only vestigial swim-bladder, it is a poor swimmer and 'hops' along, as it were. It has two dorsal fins and bare, scaleless skin.

Its colouring, which is very variable, matches its environment; on a light-coloured bed it is brownish, whereas among dark stones it may be completely black. All its fins except the ventral fins are marked with dark stripes. Its white, unmarked ventral fins are a typical feature distinguishing the Miller's Thumb from the otherwise very similar Siberian Bullhead. The innermost ray of these fins is at least half the length of the longest ray. In Europe, the Miller's Thumb is distributed from northern Spain, England and Wales as far as the river Neva in the USSR; it also occurs in southern Sweden, but is absent from most of Scandinavia and the Iberian peninsula.

The Miller's Thumb spends most of its time hiding under stones in the trout and the grayling zones and leaves its shelter only when disturbed or if it catches sight of prey in the vicinity. It spawns in April and May (at low altitudes sooner). The adult fish look for a suitable spot among the stones and the female carefully cleans it. The eggs are generally laid on the under side of stones, but sometimes in a pit in the sand on the bed. The male watches over the eggs and fans them with its fins to ensure that they have a constant supply of clean, oxygenated water. The eggs are relatively large (over 2 mm in diameter); the fry are hatched in about three weeks.

The Miller's Thumb was formerly thought to be an arch-enemy and food rival of Trout. Although it undoubtedly has a liking for trout eggs, it feeds mainly on creatures which hide under stones and in crevices, where trout would mostly be unable to reach them, and so is not in direct competition for food.

Like the Siberian Bullhead, the Miller's Thumb is a sensitive indicator of the cleanness and oxygen content of the water. Anglers sometimes use them both as bait for catching Trout.

Distribution of
C. gobio

Cottus poecilopus

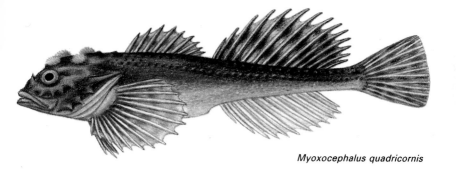
Myoxocephalus quadricornis

Siberian Bullhead
Cottus poecilopus HECKEL

▶
Bullheads, Sculpins
Cottidae

The Siberian Bullhead, which inhabits the upper reaches of rivers emptying into the Arctic Ocean, the Baltic and the Black Sea, has long ventral fins which stretch beyond the anal orifice and are marked with regular dark cross stripes. The innermost ray is much shorter than in the Miller's Thumb. Both bullheads grow to a length of 10—15 cm, but seldom more.

Their northern marine cousin *Myoxocephalus quadricornis* (L.). (the Fourhorn Sculpin) has several resident freshwater forms inhabiting Swedish lakes and Lake Onega. It usually measures about 25 cm.

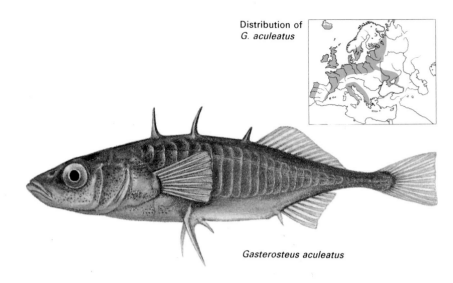

Gasterosteus aculeatus

Three-spined Stickleback
Gasterosteus aculeatus (L.)

Sticklebacks
Gasterosteidae

The Three-spined Stickleback is a tiny fish which seldom measures more than 4—6 cm. What makes it remarkable is that on its back, in front of its dorsal fin, it usually has three (though sometimes only two and sometimes up to five) separate spiny fin rays with no connecting membrane between them. Its sides are usually— though not always—covered by a longitudinal row of large bony plates; this armour is well developed on sticklebacks living in the sea, whereas fish living in fresh water are only partly armoured or not at all. The Three-spined Stickleback has a greyish green, bluish green or dark grey back and silvery sides. At spawning time, the front of the male's under side turns bright red or orange, while its belly is silvery and the whole of its body acquires a noticeable metallic lustre.

In Europe, the Three-spined Stickleback's range extends from the Iberian peninsula, Italy and the Black Sea in the south to Iceland, the northern coast of Norway and the White Sea in the north and to the Dvina, Dnepr and Crimea in the east. The fish exists in two forms—a migratory marine form and a resident freshwater form.

Spawning takes place in April and May and is sometimes prolonged into June. The male builds an untidy nest made of fragments of plants and several females lay eggs in it in turn. The male then looks after the fertilized eggs and protects the fry. The young sticklebacks remain in the nest until their yolk sac has been absorbed and then disperse into the surrounding water. They first of all live on small planktonic organisms, but later change to bottom-dwelling organisms and prey on the larvae of various insects (especially midges). Sticklebacks also devour the eggs of other fishes during the latters' spawning season. In suitable environments they often form very large populations.

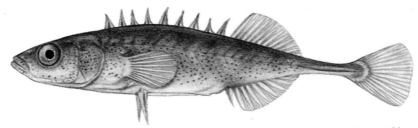

Pungitius pungitius

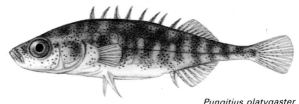

Pungitius platygaster

Nine-spined Stickleback
Pungitius pungitius (L.)

Sticklebacks
Gasterosteidae

The Nine-spined Stickleback, which measures about 7 cm, has 7—12 isolated spiny rays in front of its dorsal fin, which is likewise situated far back on its body. It is generally slimmer than the related Three-spined Stickleback and has bony plates only at the base of its caudal fin. It is a resident freshwater fish and strays just occasionally to salty water. In Europe it lives near the shores of the Arctic Ocean, the North Sea, the Baltic and the Black Sea. It has a greyish brown back and lighter sides with a metallic lustre. Dark cross stripes are present on its back and sides; at spawning time the male's throat and the front of its belly are black, while old fish are often completely black. This species frequents shallow water, where it lives near the bed; its biology is similar to that of the Three-spined Stickleback.

The Ukrainian Stickleback, *Pungitius platygaster* (Kessler) is a related species which inhabits the Black Sea, the Sea of Azov and the Aral Sea and travels up the Danube as far as Belgrade. It has 8—11 isolated spines in front of its dorsal fin.

175

Food of *Lota lota*

Burbot
Lota lota (L.)

○
Codfishes
Gadidae

The Burbot is the only freshwater representative of the cod family; the rest all live in the sea. As in other codfishes, the Burbot's ventral fins are situated well forwards, so that they lie ahead of the pectoral fins. There are no hard rays in any of the fins, but the second ray of the ventral fins is much longer than the others. In the middle of the lower jaw, on the front of the chin, there is a conspicuous fleshy barbel below the wide mouth. The Burbot has two dorsal fins—a short one in front and a very long one behind it; the anal fin is also long. Both terminate just before the beginning of the rounded caudal fin.

The Burbot usually has a brownish, brownish grey or ochre yellow body with striking dark marbled markings; young specimens are very dark. The belly is white or greyish white. The tiny, rounded scales are embedded deep in the skin, which thus gives the impression of being scaleless. In European waters the Burbot usually measures 60—80 cm and weighs 2—3 kg (rarely up to 6 kg). The largest known Burbot, caught in Germany, weighed 15 kg—probably the maximum limit for this fish.

In Europe, the Burbot is distributed eastwards from the east of England, north of the Loire, the Po and the Balkan Mountains as far as the river Ural. It also occurs on the far north, in rivers emptying into the Arctic Ocean.

L. lota

Distribution of L. lota

Lota lota

It occurs in practically all the fish zones from trout streams in the mountains to slow-flowing lowland rivers in the bream zone. In some places Burbot also live in clean ponds with water constantly flowing through them. In addition to having high oxygen requirements, they do not tolerate the slightest pollution and are therefore excellent indicators of the state of the water.

The Burbot is an essentially nocturnal fish and spends the daytime hiding under stones or overhanging banks and in similar shelters. It usually spawns in December and January, when it migrates to shallow sandy and stony water with a strong current. The female lays up to 1,000,000 small eggs, each with a large fat droplet, which drift with the current until they reach a quiet backwater, where they remain sticking to sand and stones on the bed. Spawning Burbot often collect together in such numbers

that they form huge masses of intertwined, writhing bodies. Small specimens live on crustaceans, worms and insect larvae; the adult fish are predatory and frequently attack quite large animals, such as frogs, water shrews, crayfish or large fishes.

It is interesting to note that their activity and voracity rise as the temperature of the water falls. Observations in the Lipno dam in southern Bohemia showed that the Burbot there were the most active when the water temperature fell to +3 to 0 °C. These Burbot live mainly on Perch and occasionally even on very quick and agile fish like Chub and Trout.

The Burbot is economically important chiefly in northern and eastern Europe, where its flesh and its large, fat liver are highly valued. It is also a popular fish with anglers.

177

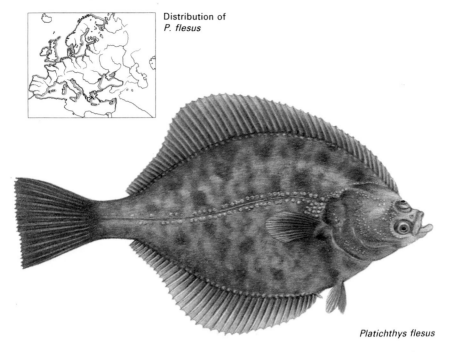

Platichthys flesus

Flounder
Platichthys flesus (L.)

○ ▷
Flatfishes
Pleuronectidae

Although flatfishes are really at home in the sea, they often migrate long distances up European rivers.

They have an extremely flattened body whose width is much greater than its height. The eyes are both situated on one side of the body, which forms the upper side and is pigmented, while the under side is white. Flatfishes have a very long dorsal and anal fin, both of which terminate very close to the caudal fin.

The most widespread of these fishes in European fresh waters is the Flounder, which is up to 45 cm long and has a brownish to olive grey upper surface adorned with frequently large, irregular black blotches and small brown or yellow spots.

The Flounder is a gregarious, shoal-forming benthic fish which prefers a sandy bed. It frequents shallow water along the shore and brackish water and it also invades rivers, often travelling long distances upstream. It occurs off every European coast from the White Sea to the Mediterranean, the Black Sea and the Sea of Azov, and over this extensive area it occurs in several closely related geographical races.

The Flounder spawns from May to April in sea-water, at depths of about 20—40 m. The eggs are pelagic and so are the fry, which are usually hatched in 5—11 days. When the young Flounders reach 8—9 mm, the shape of their body begins to change and their eyes shift to one side; at the same time they sink to the bottom and never again leave the bed. At first they live on small crusta-

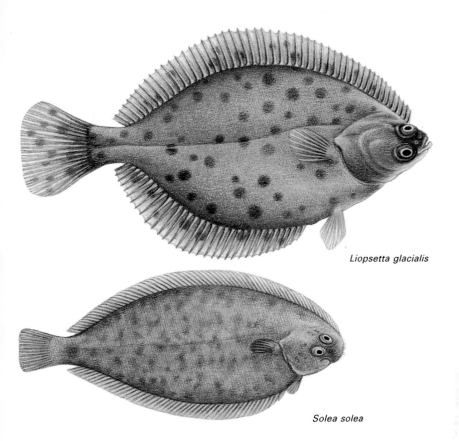

Liopsetta glacialis

Solea solea

ceans and worms; later they live mainly on molluscs and also insect larvae when they migrate up European rivers. They do not swim back to the sea again until the end of their third or fourth year. In the past, the Flounder used to be quite a common fish in the Rhine, the Elbe and other big European rivers, but water construction works and increasing pollution have put an end to these excursions once and for all. The Flounder is still an economically important fish in northern Europe, where it is caught with different types of nets and by anglers.

The Polar Flounder (*Liopsetta glacialis* Pallas) occurs in the Arctic Ocean and frequently migrates long distances up north European rivers. It grows to a length of about 20 cm (exceptionally up to 30 cm). It is interesting to note that the males of this species have ctenoid scales and the females cycloid scales. The Polar Flounder lives chiefly on small marine and freshwater molluscs. It spawns along the shores of the Arctic Ocean, mostly in May, and in the Kara Sea from Jaunary to February, at temperatures of below 0 °C. It is of relatively small and only local significance (in the rivers and seas of northern Europe).

The Dover Sole (*Solea solea* L.), another member of the Pleuronectidae family, invades European fresh and brackish water in river estuaries.

Glossary of terms

adipose fin
modified rayless dorsal fin found in Salmonid fish and a few other families.

alevin
newly hatched salmonid fish still possessing yolk sac.

anadromous
species which grow and mature in saltwater but migrate to fresh water to spawn.

benthic
bottom-dwelling.

catadromous
species which grow and mature in freshwater but which migrate to saltwater to spawn.

ctenoid
scales having a serrated margin.

cycloid
scales having a smooth margin.

littoral
shallow water round the margin of lakes etc.

operculum
bony gill cover.

parr
immature salmonid fish between the fry and smolt stages.

pelagic
zone of open water.

phytoplankton
microscopic plants present in open water.

redd
depression in sand or gravel excavated by salmonid fish for spawning.

zooplankton
microscopic animals present in open water.

Index of common names
Numbers in bold type refer to main entries

Index of scientific names

Numbers in bold type refer to main entries